Edited by Kathy Evans
Proofread by Marial Shea
Cover design by Tanya Lloyd Kyi/Spotlight Designs
Cover photograph © Getty Images
Interior design by Warren Clark

Printed and bound in Canada

National Library of Canada Cataloguing in Publication Data

Johnson, Eve
    Eating my words : how Marilyn Monroe is like a grilled artichoke
    and other observations on food / Eve Johnson.

    Includes index.
    ISBN 1-55285-505-8

    1. Food--Social aspects. 2. Food habits. 3. Cookery. I. Title.
TX355.5.J63 2003   641.3   C2003-911231-4

The publisher acknowledges the support of the Canada Council for
the Arts and the Cultural Services Branch of the Government of
British Columbia for our publishing program. We acknowledge the
financial support of the Government of Canada through the Book
Publishing Industry Development Program for our publishing
activities.

A number of registered trademarks® and trademarks™ are used in this book including
Jell-O, Certo, Cheez Whiz, Cool Whip, Miracle Whip, Minute Rice, Velveeta (Kraft Inc.);
Coke and Coca-Cola (Coca-Cola Ltd.); 7-Up (Pepsi Co. Inc.); Post-it (3M); Ferrero
Rocher (Ferrero, Inc.); Cheezies (W.T. Hawkins Ltd.); Kleenex (Kimberley-Clark
Corporation); Mars Bar (Effem, Inc.); Cheerios (General Mills Inc.). Please advise
the publisher of any omissions or corrections.

eating my words

eve johnson

Eve Johnson

December 2003

Doreen,
Something we should try
more often... having fun
with our food!
Enjoy!
With love,
Lesley
3:)

how marilyn monroe is like a grilled artichoke and other ob

eating my words

eve johnson

foreword by arthur black

whitecap

Foreword *vii*
Introduction *ix*

HOME FIRES

Kitchen Disasters *3*
Chicken with Forty Cloves of Garlic *8*
Edith Adams, Domestic Goddess *13*
The Wolf at the Door *17*
Lemon Meringue Pie *21*
Evil Spirits in the Kitchen *26*
The Four Food Groups *30*
The Celery We Knew *34*
Famous Pigs of Literature *38*
The Crotchety Old Fudge Recipe *42*
The Flaming Christmas Pudding *47*
Wood Stove *54*
Rye *59*

HUNGRY QUESTIONS

How Marilyn Monroe Is Like a Grilled Artichoke *65*
Mangoes and Sticky Rice *70*
Figs: An Appreciation *75*
Fine as Toast *79*
Hot Pepper Masochism *83*
Why Chocolate Is Evil *88*
Why Ginger Is Hot *94*
Mangoes and Apples *99*
Why Mushrooms Are Scary *103*
Medlars *108*
Pheasant Under Glass *112*
Gin: the Crack of Its Day *115*
Luwak Coffee *120*
A Mess of Pottage *124*

REAL MARSHMALLOWS
AND OTHER PARADOXES OF MODERN FOOD

Cotton Candy *131*

Ketchup *135*

Cheezies *140*

Twinkies *144*

Real Marshmallows *149*

Soda Water *153*

Fast Food *157*

Bedevilled Eggs *161*

Round Food with a Hole in the Middle *166*

The Fat of the Land Is Passé *170*

Culinary Roots *174*

Famine *178*

WORDS FOR EATING, FOOD FOR THOUGHT

Why I Quit My Job as a Restaurant Critic *185*

Losing Ten Pounds *189*

Elixirs *193*

Breatharians: Eating Air *197*

Do Men Need Meat? *201*

Satiety *205*

Eating Contests *209*

Why Backwash Is Dirty *213*

Forbidden Fruit *217*

Eating to Live or Living to Eat? *221*

Acknowledgements *225*

Index *226*

Foreword

LET ME LAY OUT MY OBJECTIVITY CREDENTIALS RIGHT OFF THE top: I don't have any. I am an unrepentant, flat-out, unabashed Eve Johnson fan.

This might be so because Eve is beautiful and witty, not to mention a great cook and a fine writer.

It might also be related to the fact that Eve showered me with free vittles for several years.

I used to be the host of a CBC radio program called *Basic Black*. One of the perks of that job was having Eve Johnson as a regular guest. Eve was *Basic Black's* Queen of Cuisine. Our Epicure of Edibles. Our Contessa of the Kitchen.

Her assignment: to find quirky, offbeat comestibles and bring them into the studio. My job was to eat them.

And what treats she brought in! Thanks to Eve, several hundred thousand CBC listeners got to listen as I tucked into mangosteens, flaming plum pudding, and a heart-stoppingly scrumptious chocolate cake that I can still taste if I close my eyes.

But it wasn't all pheasant under glass. The emphasis was on "quirky," and Eve delivered. I got to eat "a mess of pottage." Blancmange. Homemade marshmallows. And a Spanish onion sandwich slathered with peanut butter.

Which I can still taste also. Without closing my eyes.

But I digress. My purpose here is to assure you that the book you hold in your hand is more than worth the price that's printed on the cover. Eve's a seasoned journalist and a fabulous cook. What more can you ask from a food book?

—Arthur Black

Introduction

THESE ESSAYS ARE MOSTLY THE PRODUCT OF TWO HAPPY YEARS when I had everything I wanted: steady love, pleasant family duties, enough money, congenial editors, something compelling to think about, and a Saturday column in *The Vancouver Sun*. I was allowed to write about anything that caught my eye, as long as it was somehow related to food.

Every working day, I got up early and walked the fifteen minutes from my door to an undeveloped stretch of Kits Beach. I'd spend an hour or more watching birds and turning over interesting objects in the sand, and in my mind. Then I'd go home and write or do more research, then make an appearance in the office.

All that, and they paid me. I was a very happy woman, no matter how much I complained about the pain of writing. The best part of all was that after ten uncomfortable years at the newspaper, I had finally found my home.

Hired on as a Lois Lane for the features department—just the person to try sailboarding or wearing clogs with retractable roller-skate wheels—I'd been a reporter, briefly, a television critic and a visual arts critic. I never really felt like I fit.

I've cared about food since I was a child. I like to cook for other people, and some of my happiest hours have been spent eating in restaurants.

Suddenly I had a job that obliged me to read cookbooks and eat out quite a bit. I was not, strictly speaking, obliged to cook, but I did, and I took up gardening, on fire to grow my own exotic salad greens. In the food section, everything connected, including the mind and the dinner plate.

In North America, food had become news. By the late 1980s, ripples of the California food revolution generally attributed to Alice Waters and her restaurant, Chez Panisse, were washing ashore in Vancouver. At first it was the surface—the pleasures of Granville Island, the new availability of goat cheese, fresh herbs, and balsamic vinegar. But the impact of fresh, local, and organic food runs far deeper than the senses. Ecologists pointed out the costs of agricultural pollution. Organic farmers lost their hippie image and took over the cutting edge of agriculture. Militant eco-vegetarians preached the gospel of veganism.

I'd been writing for the food pages for two years when the paper's Saturday magazine was once again overhauled. They wanted quirky writing, with lots of facts, and gave me a column, no recipes required. The freedom was startling. So was the frequency with which I found myself being knocked off balance. I'd start out expecting to learn some entertaining information about arugula, for example, or figs, and then find myself in the presence of a living being, with a history, and furthermore, a personality.

Something I had always thought of as merely food turned out to be singular life form, just like me. It seemed I couldn't pick a topic that wouldn't land me in a tangled heap in the web of being.

At other times, an innocent exploration into lemon meringue pie or rye whisky wired me into the high-voltage line of childhood experience. At first this caught me by surprise, since I'd mistakenly assumed that evocative food memories belonged to members of happy families. I would start off to write about why North Americans pretend to see chocolate as evil and find myself confessing to a juvenile theft. Or I'd try to come to terms with what makes cooks ill-tempered and end up retelling the dynamic of my family dinner table. More often than I would ever have expected,

I wrote about my mother, a specialist at keeping me off balance.

If there is an air of bemusement in this book, of someone deeply puzzled and surprised, it's because I kept discovering, week after week, how quickly any food question took me back to the core—the intersection of food, sex, and religion. Gradually I realized that this was no accident or personal quirk—it's the way we're wired. Food is so central to our lives that it touches us on deep levels whether we're conscious of the touch or not.

The truth is that all that we eat is life. We are life feeding on life and we will be eaten in turn. We are gloves slipped over the hand of life. It animates us for a while and then pulls out: same inner substance, different style of glove.

Eventually I stopped writing the weekly food column and started editing the food section. My mother died. I wrote two cookbooks, was food columnist for the radio show *Basic Black*, took a leave of absence from the newspaper, and never went back. I didn't stop writing about food, and I still feel the same way about it: what we eat is our deepest connection with the world, and a connection very much worth thinking about.

These days I spend more of my time teaching yoga than I do writing, amused and bemused that yoga philosphy calls the flesh and bones we shape into poses "the food body." It seems there is no escaping food.

The stories in this book are my favourites. I think that together they convey some of the scope of the territory we traverse when we eat.

I'm happy that I'm able to put them into your hands. May they nourish you as much as they nourished me.

HOME FIRES

Kitchen Disasters

ONE EVENING, SEVERAL YEARS AGO, I HAD SOME FRIENDS OVER
for Indian food.

My apartment didn't have a dining room, so I pulled the
kitchen table out from the wall, and sat them behind it, a foot or
so away from me at the chopping block. Supper was almost ready.
I had just finished rolling chapatis. Alan, my husband, was at the
stove, cooking them. I began to shape the leftover lump of dough
by slapping it from palm to palm like a baseball. On a pass from
right to left, I overshot my hand. The dough landed in a bowl of
tomato and mushroom soup that was sitting on the table. Out of
the bowl rose a red wave that seemed to hang for a moment at its
highest point before hurling itself upon the guests.

That is a story of kitchen disaster.

Here is a story of kitchen failure. Once I made a cheese soufflé
and added only a half cup of water, instead of the one and a half
cups the dish actually required. I knew the mixture didn't look
right, because I had made soufflés before. I read and reread the
recipe, and then, against my better judgment, followed it. It turned
out there was a typographical error in the cookbook, but I didn't
find that out until after I pulled a sorry, shrunken lump out of the
oven.

In a kitchen disaster, physical reality takes an abrupt left turn

3

into the bizarre. There's always an element of accident, of surprise. Our ultimate lack of control over the outside world is demonstrated in such an overblown way that, paradoxically, it puts our fears to rest. I don't usually soak my guests in soup. I can't remember having doused anyone else with food, at least by accident, before or since. It happened once, and it would be like lightning striking twice to have it happen again.

Kitchen failure is day-to-day physical reality acted out in dreary detail. Not only has it happened once, you know it's going to happen again, just as soon as you get sloppy, or careless, or forget the perils that await the cook who values recipes over experience. The worst thing about kitchen failure is that it makes people believe they can't cook. In reality, everyone who cooks with any sense of adventure fails regularly in some way, major or minor. The best cooks in the world make mistakes and have bad days. The difference between cooks and non-cooks lies not in their failures, but in how they feel them.

Consider the enormous number of people who say they can't make bread. Some have tried and failed; others have suffered ultimate failure by never getting up the nerve to try. These people can learn to bake bread. I bake bread, and I can assure you that it's far easier than keeping your sense of direction inside buildings, or filing your tax return on time. All you really need to learn to bake bread is attitude.

Until I was seven, my mother baked every week. I would rather have eaten Sunbeam bread from the store, having fallen under the spell of the eternally happy little blue-eyed, blond-haired girl pictured on the waxed paper wrapper eating a slice of bread, an image even more powerful when you saw it larger than life on the side of a delivery truck. I wanted to know her, or possibly be her. As a second choice, I wanted to eat her bread.

But I hung around the kitchen on baking days. I watched the yeast sink to the bottom of the bowl of water and honey, soften, and then bubble and rise to the surface. I watched my mother knead the rough, wet dough into an elastic ball pumped full of energy by the heel of her hand. She used to run the ball of dough across my cheek so I could feel how soft and smooth it was when the kneading was done. Dough in the bowl, before it's been shaped, rises till it doubles. I sometimes got to punch it down, plunging my fist in up to the elbow, hearing the deep sigh of bread dough collapsing. And when we made cinnamon buns, my brother and I fought over who got to sprinkle brown sugar and cinnamon over the dough.

When I was fifteen or so, my mother gave me a few cursory bread-making lessons. She walked me through a recipe once, and answered questions after that. But I had already absorbed the most important knowledge: baking bread is no big deal. If anything, my mother handled bread dough roughly, as if she was daring it to give her trouble. More than any other kitchen activity, baking bread put her in mind of cooking for threshing crews in her prairie girlhood. Her attitude was industrial: you just made it, in quantity, often. There was nothing precious about bread, no time to waste shaping perfect loaves. She would grasp a fistful of dough, slice it off with a butcher knife, slap it into a rough oval, and drop it in a greased bread pan.

Once, when I was supplementing her bread-making lessons with a few tips from my 1967 *Robin Hood Canadian Flour Cookbook*, she caught me dividing the dough into quarters, shaping each quarter into a long rectangle exactly the width of the bread pan, then meticulously rolling the rectangle into a perfect loaf. She said: "Your grandmother would turn over in her grave to see you now."

My bread-making career is pocked with failures. I've probably made as much bad bread as most of the people who say cooking with yeast is beyond their abilities. I've baked bread with crusts that were too thick and tough as leather. I've baked refrigerator dough that refused to rise no matter how long I left it to proof in the pan. I've baked bread that broke along the side, a grotesquely swollen loaf with jagged shards of bread where the dough had burst. Exactly which law I violated is not too clear. According to

Robin Hood, the last of those imperfect loaves was either a result of using too much dough for the size of the pan, or letting it rise too long in the pan, or putting it in too slow an oven.

None of my failures ever shook my conviction that I can bake bread. My mother baked bread with confidence, and passed the confidence on to me. Like anyone, I get rusty. Baking bread regularly gives you a knowledge in the hands that is lost if you let it slide for more than a month. But once you've had the touch, it doesn't take much to get it back. Failure can't stop me, any more than it can stop any cook with confidence.

My friend Gertie Thwaites, a gentle little English woman who came to Canada with her husband shortly after the First World War, had a bread failure once that turned into a disaster. She had decided to put on a show of her domestic efficiency by making a giant batch. But the yeast was unfamiliar, the kitchen was cold, and the dough didn't rise. Gertie gave up, and rather than admitting publicly to the waste of flour, she buried the mess in the garden. Later on, the afternoon turned hot. She was out hanging clothes on the line when the ground began to move. The bread rose, and the earth with it, and it oozed out white and horrible, swelling and sighing as the air bubbles rose and burst.

Gertie used to tell that story and howl with laughter. It never held her back from baking bread.

If you're looking for a yeast recipe to get comfortable with, here's my suggestion. The food processor does the kneading—although ten minutes by hand will work just as well. It gives you the power of making lightning-fast pizzas, much better than delivery. The only tricky part is getting the right temperature for the water: too cold and the yeast will be slow to act, too hot and you'll kill it. Use a thermometer until you develop a feel for it—you may find that your hot-water tap dispenses exactly the water temperature you need.

Half of the recipe makes a pizza for two. I pop the other half in a medium freezer bag and keep it in the fridge until I need it—after several days it develops a slight whiff of sourness, and tastes even better when baked.

Fearless Pizza Dough

4 cups (1 L) all-purpose flour
2 Tbsp. (30 mL) instant yeast
2 tsp. (10 mL) salt
1 tsp. (5 mL) sugar
1^1/$_2$ cups (375 mL) water (see below for temperature)
3 Tbsp. (45 mL) olive oil

Preheat the oven to 500°F (260°C).

In a large-capacity food processor fitted with a steel blade, combine the flour, yeast, salt, and sugar. Measure the water, checking that the temperature is 125° to 130°F (50° to 55°C). Add the oil to the hot water. With the motor running, gradually pour the hot water mixture through the feed tube. Process, adding up to 2 tablespoons (25 mL) cold water until the dough forms a ball, then process for 1 minute to knead.

Turn the dough out onto a lightly floured surface. Cover with plastic wrap and let rest for 10 minutes. Divide the dough into 2 pieces. Each piece will make one 12-inch (30-cm) circle, or one 15 × 10-inch (38 × 25.5-cm) oblong—think cookie sheet. Top as desired.

Bake for 8 minutes, then slide the pizza from the pan directly on to the oven rack. Bake an additional 1 to 2 minutes or until bottoms of crusts are crisp and golden.

Chicken with Forty Cloves
of Garlic

CHICKEN WITH FORTY CLOVES OF GARLIC IS POETIC TRUTH
expressed in a recipe, a subtle meditation on the idea of enough.

I will grant you that this is not obvious from surface appearances. Chicken with forty cloves of garlic is, after all, just directions for making dinner. It was originally written in the language of Cookery, before being translated into Spanish, French, and English. Cookery is a human language too, and its poetic moments translate as satisfactorily as those of any other language, which is to say, not well at all. But live with it long enough and chicken with forty cloves of garlic will disclose its meaning, a meaning at least as profound as much of what you'll find pressed between covers under the title *Collected Poems*.

The recipe is simple: a cut-up chicken, browned in oil, is laid on a bed of garlic segments—roughly four heads' worth. Some recipes call for wine and herbs too; some don't. Salt, pepper, a tight lid, a slow oven, a few hours, and that's it. It is essential that the garlic, whether peeled or left in its skin, should not be chopped or crushed. Garlic does not give off its characteristic reek until its cell walls are broken and the sulphur in the cells forms sulphurous compounds. When garlic is roasted whole, many of the more active compounds are never created, and more are driven off in cooking. Cooked slowly, garlic becomes a soft, warm, sensual paste. Popped out of its husk and spread over a piece of bread, it has an elemental, round, nutty warmth.

Whoever first created chicken with forty cloves of garlic went to her eternal rest centuries ago. In fact, it isn't entirely clear where the dish was first eaten. American food writer John Thorne made a thorough investigation of the territory in his *Simple Cooking* newsletter. Chicken with forty cloves of garlic (*poulet aux quarante gousses d'ail*), is claimed, Thorne writes, by Provençe, Béarn, Gascony, the Dauphiné, and the Dordogne. His best guess is that the dish came originally from Catalonia, the triangular area in the northeastern corner of Spain that for much of its history has had closer ties with southeastern France than with the rest of Spain.

Its North American history began in 1963 with James Beard, the father of American gastronomy. It has been printed in *Gourmet* magazine and is commonplace enough (despite the shocked gasps you can still get from people who haven't heard of it) to turn up as a requested recipe in newspapers from time to time.

Turn from history to analysis, and the first thing you notice is this: it's always forty cloves of garlic. Not thirty-five, not thirty-nine, not forty-two. Forty. Thorne mentions a Catalan dish, *pistache de mouton*, which is a leg of mutton with fifty cloves of garlic, and garlic lover Rachael Norman won a prize at the 1989 Gilroy Garlic festival in California with a recipe for vegetarian chili with one hundred cloves of garlic. But these are the exceptions.

Forty, as anyone who has had a fortieth birthday knows, is a number vested with magical significance. The Bible is full of forties. My 1965 edition of *Brewer's Dictionary of Phrase and Fable* has this list: "Moses was forty days in the mount; Elijah was forty days fed by ravens; the rain of the flood fell forty days, and another forty days expired before Noah opened the window of the ark; forty days was the period of embalming; Nineveh had forty days to repent; Our Lord fasted forty days; He was seen forty days after His resurrection, etc."

Of the more secular forties, the one we're most familiar with now is "quarantine," from the Italian word *quaranta*, which means forty. In the Middle Ages, travellers were isolated for forty days if they had come from a plague-stricken country.

Forty can be read as either four tens or ten fours. It magnifies the sense of completion that four and ten embody. There are four directions; medieval science knew four elements—earth, air, fire, and water; medieval medicine appropriated them into a system of four bodily "humours." There are four suits in our deck of cards, and ten minor cards in each suit. Tarot, the system of divination based on the forerunners of our playing cards, assigns to ten the meaning "perfection through completion."

So forty means enough. The time elapsed may be as brief as forty winks, but if there are really forty of them we will rise from our nap feeling that we slept. Forty cloves is clearly enough garlic. But enough for what? What transformation may we expect of those forty cloves?

Ford Madox Ford, the British novelist, told what is now the best-known story of the transformative power of chicken with forty cloves of garlic in his 1935 popular history, *Provence: From Minstrels to the Machine*. A model in London loved garlic but smelled offensively of it. Her co-workers complained, and eventually she was told that she would be discharged unless she stopped her garlic habit. Plunged into despair, she went home, cooked chicken with forty cloves of garlic, and ate it with a deep sense of having made the right choice. She returned to work resigned to losing her job. But a miracle had occurred: she no longer smelled of garlic. Her co-workers complimented her on how good she looked and how nice she smelled. Ford believed that by welcoming garlic in overwhelming quantity, the model had somehow accustomed her body to it, that "the perfume of *allium officinale* attends only on those timorous creatures who have not the courage, as it were, to wallow in that vegetable."

It's a good story, but a lousy answer to what forty cloves of garlic is enough to accomplish. Only the garlic-phobic Brits are fixated on eating garlic without later smelling of it. The Catalan who first roasted forty cloves with a chicken had no such end in view.

What happens when you eat chicken with forty cloves of garlic is this: garlic, a potent aromatic, transforms into a vegetable. The plant that was widely believed to be able to neutralize a magnet, the vampire deterrent, the remedy for all diseases (according to seventeenth-century English herbalist Nicholas Culpepper), the plant that sprang up at Satan's left foot when he walked from the Garden of Eden, becomes something you can eat in quantity.

Even though the sulphur compounds are much diminished, and the roasted cloves are mild and buttery, you can still taste earthy pleasures. Garlic enthusiasts call themselves lovers of the stinking rose, not lovers of the stinking lily, even though garlic is a member of the lily family. Garlic, you see, could never really be a lily. Lilies are for purity; roses are for passion.

Thorne points out that although Ford's story of the model is usually told as a commentary on the harmless nature of cooked garlic, the true point of the story comes two hundred pages after her forty-clove epiphany, when Ford admits he "could not, in fact, bring himself to eat those garlic cloves 'as if they were haricot beans,' because he was not a hero."

Heroes undertake journeys, sometimes deep into the earth, to meet the forces of chaos and darkness. There is no food that resonates more clearly of the earth than garlic. Chicken with forty cloves of garlic says: "You've got to go back to Mother Earth." So it turns out that forty cloves of garlic is enough to meet your mother. And by definition, she's enough.

If you like finicky kitchen work, then by all means peel the garlic cloves, taking care not to bruise them. Otherwise, just separate them from the head of garlic, brushing away any extra papery skin. Once they're cooked, the garlic paste inside will squeeze out effortlessly.

You need a pan with a tight-fitting lid to retain the juices. Covering the pan with aluminum foil before you put the lid on makes a complete seal.

Chicken with Forty Cloves of Garlic

3 to 4 lbs. (1.5 to 2 kg) chicken pieces, with bones and skin
1 Tbsp. (15 mL) oil for browning, if necessary
salt and pepper to taste
40 cloves of garlic (approximately 4 heads)
$^1/_2$ cup (125 mL) chicken stock
3 large sprigs of thyme

Preheat the oven to 350°F (180°C).

On high heat, in a large, non-stick, ovenproof skillet with
a tight-fitting lid, brown the chicken on both sides, about
5 minutes per side. Season with salt and pepper. Drain off
any chicken fat that has collected.

Add the garlic cloves, peeled or unpeeled, and the chicken stock.
Lay the thyme sprigs over the chicken. Cover the skillet with
aluminum foil and fit the lid on top.

Bake in the oven for 40 to 50 minutes, or until juices from the
chicken run clear.

To serve, scoop up the garlic cloves along with the chicken. The
cooked garlic will easily squeeze out of its skin.

Edith Adams, Domestic Goddess

꧁

JUST TWO WEEKS BEFORE MARTHA STEWART TURNED HERSELF into a publicly traded corporation, Edith Adams, at 87, lost her last toehold in *The Vancouver Sun's* Wednesday food section. Any rational person would dismiss this as pure coincidence. But when it comes to Edith, I am not rational. My mom, the house I live in, and Edith all entered the world in 1912, and now only the house remains.

Edith disappeared without fanfare. She hadn't been showing up regularly in the paper anyway, so it's hard to put an exact date on her departure. The first issue of her replacement, a questions-and-answers column called "By Request," appeared on October 6, 2000.

It makes me sad, but I do understand why Edith was canned. *The Vancouver Sun* is far too sophisticated a newspaper to keep an imaginary friend on staff, no matter how long she's been around. For the sad truth is that Edith Adams never really existed, any more than Betty Crocker did. Her name was made up by a Mr. Gates, who was by some accounts an editor and by others a typesetter. He chose the name Edith Adams because it has no descenders—those parts of letters that extend below the line—a boost to the typesetter theory.

From these humble beginnings, Edith grew to be the Martha Stewart of her day. By 1947, when her "cottage"—a suite of rooms that included a fully functional kitchen—opened in the old *Sun* tower with a staff of five home economists and its own street entrance, Edith was the last word on any homemaking inquiry. It wasn't just recipes then, but how to decorate your house, plan a big party, knit, tat, crochet, get stains out of anything, and make multi-coloured Christmas "logs" out of rolled-up newspapers and chemical salts to burn in the fireplace over the holidays. Edith sponsored cooking demonstrations and, in the early 1960s, could sell out the 2,900-seat Queen Elizabeth Theatre for a demonstration of the newest advances in cooking and home appliances.

The slight absurdity of having five real women pretend to be one fictional one did not go unnoticed. In 1966, columnist Paul St. Pierre felt called upon to explain that "When *The Sun* advises readers to ask Edith Adams it is like an Arab sheikh saying 'Meet my wife.' There are many girls there. They are Enid Adam, Dawn Adam, Isobel Adam, Theresa Adam and Helen Adam, and we don't know what we're going to do if one gets married."

Home economist Brenda Thompson is the last remaining member of the food section to have answered the phone as Edith. Like all of the Ediths, Brenda is a practical woman. "When a person dies, no matter how hard it is, you eventually have to move on," she says. "Edith was never even alive. Get over it."

I will, of course. But not before saying goodbye. And not before I point out that Martha and Edith, in relation to each other, say meaningful things about the world we live in and the one we've left behind. Yes, they are both homemaking authorities with old-fashioned names. But Edith functioned on the scale of the city. You could get closer to Edith, who didn't really exist, than you can to Martha, who does.

Martha is a continent-wide phenomenon. But no matter how many times you see her on TV, it would be a waste of time to call her up in the midst of jelly making to find out why the damned stuff won't set. You can, it's true, connect with an editor of one of Martha's publications on her web site—for a prescheduled talk on a predetermined subject, but somehow it's not the same.

And how real is Martha anyway? When we read her calendar for November 7 and find that she plans to "turn off outdoor faucets and chicken-house water," we know that Martha does not inhabit the same world we do. We're just puzzled spectators, asking: What are the chickens supposed to drink now? Is it possible that (gulp) the chickens are soup, and next spring there'll be new chickens?

Martha promises the joy of homemaking. Edith helped with the job of homemaking. Martha suggests that we restore our own cane chairs, make "turkey trivia" place cards for Thanksgiving dinner, buy fabric and make our own theme napkins for a baby shower. Edith's world had families to feed on a limited budget, stains to remove, and green beans to can.

Edith's goal was to help you feel adequate, up to the task. It seems to me that Martha's is the reverse: she demonstrates how inadequate you truly are, and therefore how much you need to buy her cookbooks and magazines, watch her television show, and visit her Web site. Even though she wasn't, no one ever thought to ask if Edith Adams was living. As far as I know, there were no spoofs of Edith. There was a bit of gentle ribbing, yes, and I'm as guilty of making Edith jokes as anyone else. My favourite was pretending to have sighted the inebriated ghost of Edith, drifting through the department with a can of cream of mushroom soup clutched in her spectral hand.

Edith has had the dwindles for some time now. She lost her separate entrance when *The Sun* moved. In 1979, after a prolonged newspaper strike, which was clearly none of her doing, Edith, whose byline once ran under every story in the food pages, was relegated to "Edith Adams Answers."

I never answered the phone as Edith, but I did, off and on for ten years, write her "Answers" and, truth be told, many of her questions, too. We were always happy to use a real letter if we could, but the odds were against us. One of the week's three recipes had to have a picture, which could be hard to get. All of them had to be in season. And while Edith had plenty of mail, much of it asked for advice too specific to frame as a general question. Other letters asked for recipes that had already been reprinted a hundred times, or for recipes you never wanted to see in print again—the ones with lime Jell-O and rainbow mini-marshmallows.

Over the years, Edith gradually came to have a fusty, behind-the-times air. Those who feel affection toward her, like Pat Pederson, an Edith for 23 years, tend to think of her as "dear Edith."

Will Martha some day become fusty and out of date? The people who bought shares in her presumably don't think so. I'm inclined to agree with them, at least in the short term. Money is an essential part of Martha's package. No one is ever going to smile patronizingly at her estate in East Hampton, or even at a life that allows you to keep chickens without having to scrub out the hen house, whether you pencil it in your Daytimer every month or not.

The Wolf at the Door

THIS SUMMER, I HAVE DECIDED TO ABANDON JAM MAKING, TO put up not so much as a batch of blackberries, fragrant with sun, against a dark, wet January morning. I can't swear that I won't cave in, late in August, wanting just one breath of a hot kitchen smelling of sugar and fruit. But a tub of blackberry pulp from last year still sits in my freezer, and three jars of last year's raspberry jam wait in the cupboard, mute testimony to the fact that at our house we don't eat toast and jam for breakfast any more.

What I'm going to miss most about jam making is my brief yearly communion with that giant of the kitchen, the mythic Mother Preserver, and her faithful companion, the Wolf at the Door.

I ran across the Mother Preserver recently while reading Susan Puckett's book, *A Cook's Tour of Iowa*. In this instance, her name is Rosemary Braun, and she's a farmwife in northwest Iowa. Braun raised twelve children on the produce from her garden. In the fall, assisted by a crew of daughters, she put up 75 quarts of green beans, 50 quarts of whole tomatoes, 100 quarts of sweet corn, 100 pounds of potatoes, and all of the berries from six beds of raspberries and strawberries.

My grandmothers, each of whom raised seven children, also gardened and canned, enough to take their families through an

Alberta winter. They didn't have a choice. What's remarkable is that they had the technology.

People have always preserved food, by salting, drying, pickling, smoke curing. But canning goes back less than two hundred years, to 1809, when Nicholas Appert, a French chef, confectioner, and distiller, picked up a 12,000-franc prize from the French Directory, the government of that time, for a startling discovery.

After fourteen years of experimenting, Appert had learned how to preserve food by enclosing it in hermetically sealed glass containers—a particularly welcome bit of news for Napoleon, who wanted a way to supply his troops with food that wouldn't rot.

Appert's discovery, published in 1811 as *L'Art de conserver, pendant plusieurs années, toutes les substances animales et végétales* (The Art of Preserving All Kinds of Animal and Vegetable Substances for Several Years), quickly spread. Commercial canners soon adopted tin as a better packaging material than glass. For home canners, the significant date in the history of canning is 1858, when New York glass-blower John L. Mason took out a patent for the Mason jar, the first glass jar with a metal, screw-on cap.

Canning companies and home canners alike often stumbled on the way to perfecting the process. Appert filled glass jars with food, heated them in boiling water, then sealed them with cork, which was reinforced with wire and sealing wax. He believed that it was contact with air that caused food to spoil.

Not until Louis Pasteur's research into micro-organisms in the 1860s did we learn why canned food could be deadly—several strains of bacteria, including *Clostridium botulinum*, which produces an often fatal form of food poisoning called botulism, flourish in sealed containers and can only be destroyed by temperatures well above the boiling point of water.

But by the turn of the century, we had reached the apogee of home canning, when every farmwife, and every frugal urban housewife, put up enough of summer's crop to feed her family for a year. It was a Herculean task, exacerbated by the fact that everything comes ripe at once. The city housewife laboured over peaches and blackberries, beans, corn, and tomatoes all threatening imminent rot if not dealt with immediately. I have faced my own moments of canning burnout, late on a hot summer night, with berries starting to mould, and something crucial missing—sugar, Certo, jars, paraffin to seal them, or, worse, the will to continue.

For the farmwife, the peak of canning season came at the same time as the grain harvest. E.B. White pointed out the hazards involved in his review of a 1940s guide to self-sufficiency called *Practical Farming for Beginners*, by H.A. Highstone. "Mr. Highstone actually suggests that the subsistence family harvest its own grain crop by mowing it with a mowing machine and making sheaves by hand," White writes. "Remember that the grain harvest is 10 tons, or 200 sacks of grain each weighing 100 pounds. And remember also that the grain harvest comes at the same season as the canning—those 600 Mason jars that have to be filled. It would take a large family of stalwart sons and daughters to put through that program without cracking. Some of the jars are going to crack, even if the children don't."

What made it worthwhile was hunger. In the 1840s, an average British working-class family of two adults and three children subsisted on this weekly diet: five four-pound loaves of bread, five pounds of meat, seven pints of beer, forty pounds of potatoes, three ounces of tea, one pound of sugar, and one pound of butter.

North America was a land of plenty in comparison, but even in the new world, fresh food couldn't be kept fresh for long. Well into the twentieth century, canned foods were luxury items. In 1913, when factory wages were $10 a week for women and $15 for men, Eaton's was selling a dozen cans of peaches for $2. What you didn't preserve, you couldn't afford to buy.

Rosemary Braun's 75 quarts of canned green beans start to look pretty good under the circumstances. So, for that matter, do the jars of home-canned raspberries that I was always being sent to the basement to fetch. My father, a prairie boy who was twenty years old in 1930, thought them a delicacy. Not having met the Wolf, I despised them, the same way I despised canned grapes in fruit salad.

Fresh raspberries are now flown in from New Zealand in the middle of the winter. They cost a lot, and seem, like all imported produce, a little tired from the journey. But there they are, along with grapes, bananas, broccoli, cauliflower and a host of other fresh things to eat. It doesn't take many jars of canned vegetables wintering over on the shelves to reveal the truth: the family would rather eat them fresh, or as a second choice, frozen.

Putting by a year's supply of food is something that most of us leave to the Mormons, or to the readers of *Harrowsmith* and similar magazines who have opted for country living on less cash, more labour, and, quite possibly, more satisfaction. We go to the market and marvel over the fresh fruit in mid-winter, stored for us, transported for us, even genetically engineered for storage and transport. The flaw, of course, is that we are less self-sufficient than ever, more at the mercy of a food system that so far has shown only a benign face of freshness and plenty—for those who can pay the price.

We have succeeded in driving off the Wolf, and shouldn't be surprised that the Mother Preserver has gone with him. They were always a pair. If some summer weekend finds us in a hot kitchen full with the smell of sugar and fruit, it will be because we want to be there, not because we feel a warm breath on the backs of our necks.

Lemon Meringue Pie

ALMOST EVERY KITCHEN HOLDS THE INGREDIENTS FOR LEMON meringue pie, almost all the time: eggs, lemon, butter, sugar, cornstarch, and a pie shell. Homey and humble, it fails in each of the three categories proposed by Roz Chast in her Young Professional Recipe Test cartoon: "Does recipe contain at least four different kinds of 'flavoured vinegars'? Does it require one tremendously expensive ingredient that you will use just this once and never again for as long as you live? Do you have to go out and buy a type of pan you've never even heard of?"

When you make lemon meringue pie, you first decide to work with what is. Then you embark on an intrinsically satisfying and meaningful process. Let's assume the existence of a pre-baked pie shell. To make lemon meringue pie, we begin by separating the eggs. Then we take the yolk (where the fat of the egg, and most of its flavour, resides) sweeten it, flavour it with a clean splash of lemon juice and a generous grating of rind, cook it with cornstarch and water, and, for good fatty measure, add a tablespoon or two of butter.

The yellow colour of the lemon pie comes from the egg, by the way, not the lemon. If you use free-range eggs your custard will be brighter yellow, and free of any taint that may cling to the products of a caged egg machine.

We beat the "white" of the egg—which in its natural state is not white at all, but clear—with sugar and cream of tartar until it forms stiff, but not dry, peaks, glossy and white as snow. Then we bake it, so that the white foam is set and captured, at least for a day or two.

Lemon meringue pie has its cooking danger zones, mostly in the area of the meringue. Overbeat the egg whites and the meringue will weep, giving off little beads of moisture that you may dab away, if you are so inclined, like beads of sweat on an upper lip. It will also weep if you underbeat the egg whites and if you store it too long in the fridge. The custard has perils of its own. "My mother thinks it's lumpy because I cook it too long. My husband thinks it gets watery because I put it in the icebox," wailed one desperate home cook to the authors of *Joy of Cooking*, who responded, with scant comfort: "How right, unfortunately, are both of this bride's critics!"

But for the most part, lemon meringue pie is cooking as alchemy: separate the *prima material*, the egg, into its two parts, intensify their distinctive qualities, and then combine them again in a greater whole. It is no wonder that the pie that results from these efforts radiates contentment.

For people who grew up eating food from North American kitchens, lemon meringue pie means contentment on a personal level too.

As a child I had two favourite desserts: anything chocolate, and lemon meringue pie. To come home from school and find lemon meringue pie meant more than just the promise of dessert once the meat and potatoes were eaten. It meant coming home to a mother who had been happy and unharried enough to engage in making this supremely unnecessary, more than a little tricky, very ephemeral pie.

Search your memory and I think you will find the same thing. So I expect that you too may share my concern that lemon meringue pie has fallen out of favour and may one day be forgotten. You will not find lemon meringue pie in cutting-edge restaurants, and it is rarely made by home cooks who have moved on to more sophisticated challenges, when they are stirred to make dessert at all. It survives in diners and department store restaurants and is almost always disappointing.

The nub of the lemon meringue pie problem is this: we have all heard, many times, that food is love. To cook for someone is to say I love you. What is more rarely pressed upon us is the range of meaning that can ride with those three simple words. Our habit is to connect food and love in two ways: mothering and passion. Any food that fits into the exhortation "Eat your lovely _____, dear, Mommy wants you to be big and strong," connects us with mother love: porridge, beef stew, broccoli, peas.

Another whole group of foods, the ones with reputations as aphrodisiacs, connects us with erotic love. Passionate food doesn't need to be as flagrant as pale, sweet, foamy, body-temperature zabaglione—one glass, two spoons—but it can be. Oysters are renowned for their erotic power. So are truffles; so is chocolate.

Lemon meringue pies fit neither category. Mothers may make them, but they are not mommy food. They are frills, desserts, things to eat for the pleasure of eating. Lovers may like them, but lemon meringue pies are too homey, too innocent and sunny, too round and wholesome to light the fires of lust. What lemon meringue pies ignite is a sense of sunny well-being. The cook who sets a lemon meringue pie to cool on the kitchen counter says: "I was happy today, so I made us something frothy to eat." Lemon meringue pie speaks the language of contented love.

For that reason, it is inescapably sad to realize that, like everything else, lemon meringue pie is just a bubble in the stream. Nothing lasts, and lemon meringue pie is set to burst quicker than most foods do, after a mere two hundred-year flicker.

Mrs. Elizabeth Goodfellow, who ran a bakeshop in Philadelphia, made the first lemon meringue pie sometime in the first half of the nineteenth century. Cooks had been making custard pies since Roman times. The Romans didn't have lemons, but the British did; by 1494 lemons were being grown in the Azores and shipped to England. Mrs. Goodfellow's genius was to combine meringue and lemon pudding in a pie shell, a distinctly American touch. It was a hit.

"Mrs. Goodfellow's pudding, now known as lemon meringue pie, was at one time a mark of great luxury in the high cookery of Philadelphia and New York, requiring as it did many fresh eggs, sweet-cream butter and fresh lemons—and thus considerable expense," writes food historian William Woys Weaver in *America Eats: Forms of Edible Folk Art* (written to accompany an exhibition of American folk cookery implements at the Museum of American Folk Art in New York in 1989).

Eliza Leslie, who was not only Elizabeth Goodfellow's protégé, but also a prolific author of cookbooks, made sure the recipe spread. There were two responses. Less generous and less affluent cooks—many of them operating boarding houses in the Midwest—reduced the lemon's role to a bit of rind and substituted vinegar for the lemon juice. We made a vinegar pie in *The Vancouver Sun's* test kitchen. It was rather good, unless you compared it to lemon meringue pie, in which case it was a travesty.

Home cooks seized upon the opportunity to say: "I was happy, so I made something frothy for us to eat." By the turn of the century, lemon meringue pie was a North American standard, a recipe you would find in every general cookbook and on almost every dinner table.

How long has it been since you made a lemon meringue pie? Contented love is now more apt to say: "I was happy, so I bought something frothy for us to eat." If in fifty years there isn't a soul alive who sees a lemon meringue pie and feels contentment, does that mean we have lost part of our vocabulary?

As it turns out I don't make lemon meringue pie much these days myself, and have no special insight into making it, but these ice-cream bars are really good, easy, make a lot, and will keep three months in the freezer.

Lemon Ice-Cream Bars Dipped in Dark Chocolate

$^1/_2$ cup (125 mL) lemon juice (about 3 lemons)
1 Tbsp. (15 mL) finely grated lemon zest
$^1/_2$ cup (125 mL) sugar
$^1/_2$ cup (125 mL) butter
$^1/_2$ cup (125 mL) whipping cream
6 egg yolks
1 13 × 9-inch (33 × 23-cm) sponge cake, 1-inch (2.5-cm) thick
3 cups (750 mL) vanilla ice cream
10 oz. (300 g) bittersweet chocolate, melted

In a medium saucepan, heat the lemon juice, lemon zest, sugar, butter, and whipping cream until the butter has melted. In a medium-sized bowl, beat the egg yolks. Whisk in a bit of the hot lemon liquid, then gradually whisk in the rest. Return to the saucepan and heat on medium until thickened, stirring constantly, about 5 minutes. Strain through a fine sieve into a bowl. Let cool.

Cut the cake into two 9 × 6 $^1/_2$-inch (23 × 15-cm) pieces. Then cut each piece in half horizontally, to make four 9 × 6$^1/_2$-inch (23 × 15-cm) sheets, each $^1/_2$ inch (1 cm) thick.

Soften the ice cream in the fridge for 20 minutes or microwave for 20 seconds. Mix with the lemon curd. If the mixture is too soft to spread, return it to the freezer for 30 minutes, stirring occasionally. When it will hold its shape, spread a $^3/_4$-inch (2-cm) thick layer over the bottom surfaces of the cakes. Replace the top layers of cakes and press down. Return to the freezer for half an hour.

With a sharp knife, cut each rectangle in half lengthwise. Then cut each 9 × 3$^1/_4$-inch (23 × 8-cm) rectangle crosswise into four equal bars.

Line a cookie sheet with waxed paper. Dip one end of each ice cream sandwich into the melted chocolate about a third of the way up, then place it on the waxed paper. Return bars to the freezer until the chocolate is set and the ice cream is completely hardened, about 30 minutes.

To store: Wrap the sandwiches individually in plastic wrap, then overwrap in freezer paper. Freeze for up to 3 months.

Makes 16 bars.

Evil Spirits in the Kitchen

RATTLE THOSE POTS AND PANS, SLAM THOSE CUPBOARD DOORS, and, in the ultimate moment of rage, smash an old plate or two—it's expected. No other place offers quite the same chance to make a lot of hostile noise while engaged in a cause as morally impeccable as getting food on the table.

We don't remark on the frequency of sudden angry fits that occur in the kitchen because they're traditional. If we looked more closely at kitchen tantrums, I suspect we would find that many of them are caused by a buildup of rage as stubborn as yellow wax on a linoleum floor—in other words, by evil spirits.

It isn't hard to see where the rage came from in the first place. Hot, dirty and ill-designed, the kitchen was the scene of hard physical labour, with never a food processor to purée the soup. Before the age of reliable stoves, any good cook knew how to judge the temperature of the oven by sticking a hand in and counting. Imagine doing that when you've just caught the cat eating butter tarts, or had a few sharp words with your lifetime companion.

Even in the most modern and best-designed kitchen, the cook suffers a lifetime of daily insults: nicks, cuts, burns, sulphuric acid from an onion tearing at the moist surface of the eyes. Lemons alone can trigger fury. It isn't just the chance scrape of the knuckles across the grater, but the juice itself. Citric acid, as Henry Beard and Roy McKie's *Cooking: A Cook's Dictionary* puts it, is "a useful substance that helps cooks to quickly locate temporarily misplaced cuts, nicks and abrasions on their fingers."

Survive the physical onslaught with equanimity intact, and the kitchen will proceed to rub your face in the sad truth of the physical world. The more fresh food you cook, the more intimate your knowledge of rot and decay becomes. Something is always getting ripe or going bad, and action will have to be taken. Who wants to plan their meals in constant awareness of that unused bit of broccoli yellowing in the back of the vegetable crisper? But cooks who don't hold decay in mind will come up against mould on the yogurt, and cucumbers turned to liquid in the bottom of the vegetable crisper.

Bruised about the hands, teary-eyed from chopping onions, and in constant sober awareness of the fleeting life of food, the cook turns outward and finds an audience that is never quite appreciative enough.

Cooking is largely unrecognized as an art. This is in part because the nature of good cooking is to leave no visible trace behind. The only lasting edifice a family's cook may build is the health of the people he or she feeds. And that's a teetery edifice, because so many other causes, from a runaway truck to industrial pollution, can topple it. It's especially hard to see the art in cooking if you have to be your own sous-chef. The cook's job description is as lofty as you could want it to be, calling as it does for a kitchen-artist and nurturing force in the home. It turns out that what you actually do is peel a lot of carrots.

Most cooks peel their carrots in isolation. A painter rejected by a gallery can turn to other artists for moral support. The cook who faces a family of boors, of people with no interest in food, of culinary Jesuits who can't possibly try anything they haven't been eating since before the age of six, has no such support group. The cook's just rage over lack of appreciation reaches its highest pitch when the ungrateful wretches we cook for don't even do us the courtesy of sitting down at the table while dinner's still hot.

No wonder kitchens are such feeding grounds for evil spirits. They grow like the bruise on a dropped apple. Each evil spirit is tailored to the cook's circumstances. In some kitchens they are strong enough to impose their own constant weather pattern—low rumblings of thunder, high winds, sudden shocking flashes of lightning.

I used to have an evil spirit living in my kitchen cupboards, one I brought with me when I left home. It was a sleek, fat thing, amply fed by the peculiar difficulties of our family dinner table. My father was always late for dinner. He was not making a statement about my mother's cooking. He was even-handedly late for everything. Two hours with a carburetor passed for him like ten minutes. A chat with the next-door neighbours could flow so fast that forty minutes disappeared in what he thought was five. Most suppertimes, his absorption in the mysteries of the automobile ran headlong into my mother's reasonable desire to have everyone arrive at the dinner table at roughly the same time.

From this conflict was born the noisy drama of calling Dad for dinner. As the messenger, I had a small but busy part. Back and forth, down the kitchen stairs along the backyard sidewalk to the garage, and back to the kitchen again. Stormy weather was brewing in both places.

When I took sides, it was with my mother. Unlike my brother, I liked the kitchen better than the garage. Besides, I could see that dinner, when the meat, the potatoes, and all the vegetables were ready at once, when the bread and the salt and pepper had been put on the table, when the margarine was out of the fridge and the table was set, had a presence, a kind of spirit. You could watch its goodness dissipate in the steam rising from the cooling plates. Every cook knows that there are dinners that will never taste as good again as in the five minutes after they arrive, balanced and whole, on the table.

If I kept my evil spirit longer than I needed to, it's because for a long time I didn't know it was there. But I like to spend time seeing what my childhood looks like from the point of view of a grownup. One day, while drifting around in my memories of home and kitchen during the vast stretches of the 1950s, I caught a fleeting glimpse of the evil spirit slipping away behind a cupboard door. Being seen was the beginning of its end.

I've stopped cooking meals that have to be eaten right away, except when we have company for dinner. I believe that if you ask someone for dinner, you have every right to expect they'll come to the table when called. For the rest, I make food that can be served at any temperature. As far as I'm concerned, antipasto plates are Italy's major contribution to world peace.

And if I find mould on the cheese or a rotted ex-avocado at the bottom of the fruit bowl, I try not to take it personally.

I would like to tell you that I've thrown my evil spirit out with the garbage, or that I caught it off guard one day and vacuumed it up. The truth is that if I drop a spice jar on a bare toe I will hop around shouting with rage as readily as anyone else. But these days, I win more rounds than the evil spirit does. It's hungry, I think, and not finding much to eat. I am confident that one day I'll see its back, slipping out the door, looking for a new home.

The Four Food Groups

❦

OKAY, CALL ME A SENTIMENTAL FOOL, BUT I DON'T LIKE IT THAT
we waved goodbye to the four food groups, and nobody even threw
them a party. Sure, they were dull, but they've been fixtures in our
image banks for years.

Close your eyes and you can see the venerable food wheel: a
cross inside a circle with one kind of food in each of the quadrants:
dairy products, meats, fruits and vegetables, and grains. It used to
be an important image—an official image. It was, after all, what
the federal government wanted your brain to register when you
heard the words "balanced diet." But the food wheel is not the official picture any more. There's a new image, and the old posters
went out with the trash.

The change came because the old image gave undue visual
emphasis to meat and dairy products, which are low in fibre and
can be high in saturated fats. We now believe that high-fat, low-
fibre diets are directly linked to heart disease, cancer, diabetes, and
strokes. In the U.S., the food pyramid replaced the food wheel. In
Canada, the new image is a rainbow, with each food group getting
its own band of colour, and taking up an equivalent amount of
rainbow space to the proportion it should appear in our diets.

I can't help having mixed feelings about this. My father died of
a heart attack that may or may not have been caused in part by his

officially sanctioned meat-and-potatoes diet. And yet I've got a soft spot for the food wheel, and the four food groups.

There's no denying that change brought loss. Have you ever heard a food rainbow joke? Yet the four food groups were a constant comic inspiration. Remember the Roz Chast cartoon? Junk food, health food, party food, and normal food, as I recall. And then there's Henry Beard and Roy McKie in their *Cooking: A Cook's Dictionary*: "There are basically four broad categories of food: carbohydrates, fats, proteins and individually wrapped chocolates with cherry centres."

More than that, the food wheel was a rare modern statement of an ancient and powerful combination of symbols. The cross represents the four elements of the world united at the fifth point, the centre. The circle is a symbol of wholeness and perfection. Jung called the cross inside a circle "an organizing scheme par excellence, something like the crossed threads of a telescope," and wrote that it is used "almost instinctively for dividing up and arranging a chaotic multiplicity"—like the world of food.

So we have four seasons, four directions, four winds. In pre-modern science there were four elements: earth, air, fire, and water. Pre-modern medicine had four humours: choleric, melancholic, sanguine, and phlegmatic. Four rivers of paradise meet to form a cross and define the four quarters of the earth. There are four suits in a deck of cards. And there are four food groups.

The directions still look firm, even if the seasons have turned a little shaky. But the four food groups are gone. In 1981, Sweden adopted eight food groups, a number arrived at by emphasizing vegetables. Fruits and berries make up one category; green vegetables and legumes another; carrots, beetroot, turnips, and swedes, a third; and potatoes a fourth. The other categories are meat, fish, and eggs; bread and other cereal products; milk and cheese; and edible fats. The British, too, have eight food groups: cereals, meat, milk and butter, fruit and vegetables, non-dairy fats, preserves, confectionery, and alcohol drinks. Yes, in Britain, candies, jam, and alcohol are food groups.

The Australians, the Americans, and the New Zealanders eat their food in five groups, although in each case there are four substantial groups and an "other" category tacked on the end. In Australia, it's butter or table margarine. In the U.S., it's fats, sweets, and alcohol. In New Zealand, it's fats, oils, sugar, jam and honey—no surprise, those last, to anyone who's set eyes on the land of the long white cloud formed from the steam of perpetually boiling teakettles.

The food wheel is the kind of symbol that sticks in a child's mind. It says: The proper balance is to eat all of these foods in equal amounts, and to eat from every group at least once a day, and better yet, once every meal. Vegetarians, it says, miss an entire quarter of a balanced diet. And it says that vegans (vegetarians who don't eat dairy products or eggs) miss half of all you need to be strong and healthy.

The problem is that it's been years since the wheel matched the fine print. Recommended numbers of daily servings laid out something graphically closer to a peace sign: six servings of grains and six of fruits and vegetables every day, with five servings from meat and dairy combined.

Gradually the four food groups became tainted by charges that, far from an honest attempt to subdue the chaos of food, they were actually a sales tool of the meat and dairy industry. The circumstances of their departure did nothing to clear their name.

In 1992, nutritionists at the U.S. Department of Agriculture (USDA) unveiled a new diagram: the Eating Right Pyramid. Bread, cereal, rice, grains, and pasta make up the base; fruits and vegetables the next level; meat and dairy the next; and finally, at the tip of the pyramid, fats, oils, and sweets. The nutritional advice was the same as that which accompanied the old food wheel. But the visual impact was entirely different.

The meat and dairy industries protested. A spokesperson for the National Cattlemen's Association told *The New York Times*: "We wanted to be sure that consumers did not misrepresent the pyramid to be a ranking of food . . . we wanted to avoid a goodfood/bad-food ranking and the de-emphasis of meat." Later the same month, the USDA announced that the release of the pyramid was being delayed indefinitely to allow for testing of the graphic on children.

North of the border, we adopted a rainbow—symbol of the bridge between this world and paradise, to name only one of its meanings. Among the "partners" who helped Health Canada decide on exactly how the rainbow ought to look were: the Beef Information Centre, the Canadian Egg Marketing Agency, and the Dairy Bureau of Canada. They can be distinguished from other "partners," like the Canadian Diabetic Association and the Canadian Nurses Association, by the fact that they have something to sell.

I like to think of the food wheel as it was back in the early days, when the main problem in nutrition was getting enough. No one saw a problem with the industry associations promoting their products in schools because meat, eggs, milk, and cheese were a whopping half of the circle. Now we battle the diseases of too much, and the symbol of our best knowledge at the time has to go. What makes me nervous is wondering what else we don't know.

The Celery We Knew

HERE'S ONE THING I KNOW ABOUT ETERNAL VERITIES: DON'T LOOK at them too closely if you want to go on thinking of them as eternal.

Consider, for example, the celery you've been eating since you were a child: omnipresent, unchanging, classic in form, as stable a vegetable as you can readily imagine. In my naïveté, I have always imagined that this celery was merely what God intended it to be—an innocuous vegetable that small children could eat before dinner without spoiling their appetites. Little did I know that my celery sticks were as much a child of the '50s as I am.

Eternal, unchanging celery turns out to be a genetic mutation discovered by plant breeder Phillip E. (Gene) Hill and first marketed by the Ferry Morse Seed Company, then of Mountain View, California, in 1952. It was called by the cosy name Utah 52-70.

For the past forty years, it has been a staple. My mother's kitchen would have been as likely to be without salt or flour as without celery, to eat raw, to chop and sauté with onions and carrots as the base note of everything from beef stew and chicken fricassee to turkey dressing and sautéed pork chops. *Sic transit gloria mundi.* On the evidence of my vegetable crisper, Utah 52-70 is on the skids.

Weeks go by without a single stalk of celery finding its way home from the market. I buy it to make chicken stock, or because a recipe I want to try calls for it, but I never come home from the market with a bunch of celery that stole my heart and demanded to be bought, the way new potatoes might, or green beans.

I do, however, buy fennel, an Italian cousin of celery, grouped on the same page in my *Oxford Book of Food Plants*, under "umbellifers grown for their leaf stems." Fennel is by far the more elegant of the two. Its white bulb shades to pale green, its dark, feathery leaves at the top of the stalks look like lacy seaweed. Its taste is tinged with anise. I eat fennel with sun-dried black olives, with creamy gorgonzola, and with smoked salmon and cream cheese. It wouldn't cross my mind to exchange it for the thin pleasures of celery.

Abandoning celery has given me a pang or two of guilt. What kind of cook, after all, spurns an eternal verity of the home kitchen in order to embrace a fancy, upstart Italian? A traditional cook, as it turns out. Fennel is by far the older vegetable, known to the Greeks and Romans, and eaten by the Italians for as long as anyone can remember. Celery, on the other hand, was a parvenu among vegetables even before Utah 52-70 rolled out of California. No one ate celery stalks at all until the seventeenth century.

The ancient and medieval world valued smallage, the wild form of celery from which our varieties derive, for its seeds. Brewed into tea, they are a powerful opiate. Our first record of celery on a dinner table dates only from 1623. Here is the best conjecture we have of what happened: A French gardener, practising selective breeding in the hopes of improving the celery seed crop, stumbled across a mutation in the garden. Instead of the hollow bitter stalk that smallage usually produced, the new plant had a solid, edible stalk.

Plant breeders gradually created two kinds of celery: yellow and green. It was available from November through January. By the 1920s, almost all of the celery grown in North America was yellow celery, blanched by piling dirt, paper, or boards around the stalks to hide them from sunlight. Blanching made the celery more tender. Then, in the 1930s, a group of celery farmers near Ogden, Utah, started growing a special, unblanched, less stringy, green celery, and sold it to chefs on the intercontinental trains that stopped in Ogden. Green celery, as served in the dining car, took on a gastronomic cachet.

The famous Utah green celery of the 1930s was not celery as we know it now. It grew 20 cm (eight inches) from the base to the joint, which is what celery growers call the part where the stalks branch out. The petioles, or leaf stalks, fanned out at the base, the way the leaf stalks of Florence fennel do now. The whole plant was between 36 and 40 cm (14 and 16 inches) tall when sold, roughly half stalk and half leafy greenery. There were only six or seven stalks in a head, and it was stringy. You couldn't just cut a stalk of celery and eat it; you had to string it first.

Blanched celery disappeared from North American tables when the U.S. entered the Second World War and American growers no longer had cheap labour. It was already falling out of favour: vitamins had given green vegetables a new prestige. Seed companies and plant breeders, meanwhile, had a new problem. The traditional growing areas were turning into cities. But celery planted in the soils of the Salinas and Oxnard Valleys, where 70 per cent of the U.S. celery crop is grown today, took on an unattractive brown colour at the centre of the stalk. The soil, Gene Hill says, was deficient in boron, a widespread semi-metallic element that is essential for plant growth. When he planted out some seeds from a Utah farmer, he was looking for a celery variety that could withstand boron-deficient soils.

It was just Cheez Whiz on the stalk that Utah 52-70, a mutant capable of thriving in Salinas, was also tall, succulent, and non-stringy, with a tight head and more stalks. Utah 52-70 grew stalks that were 28 cm (11 inches) long before the joint, that grouped together tightly and provided a dozen stalks in a single head. Produce buyers were skeptical at first. "They thought it didn't look good because it had a short, stubby top," Hill says. But it took just over a year for Utah 52-70 to become the industry standard.

Ever since 1952, plant breeders have been adapting Utah 52-70 to different soils, extending its season so that somewhere in California it is always time to be growing celery, and looking for resistant varieties to counter disease. They always return to Utah 52-70's "phenotype"—that is, they cross whatever resistance to heat, cold, or disease they are working on with a Utah 52-70 variety, so the resulting celery will look like the same pale green troughs we filled with Cheez Whiz, and chopped into Waldorf salads.

The green celery that was such a hit on the transcontinental trains became the kitchen staple of the '50s and '60s. It may now be the forgotten vegetable of the '90s. I don't remember the last time I was offered celery as an appetizer in any restaurant that believes itself to be within fifty yards of the cutting edge. Check out the new cookbooks and you'll find more recipes for celeriac, the knobbly celery-flavoured root, than you will for celery. *Chez Panisse Cooking*, by Paul Bertolli with Alice Waters, has two fennel recipes. Celery doesn't even appear in the index.

Live by fashion, die by fashion. Right now we are raising a generation of children to whom kiwi fruit always was and always will be. I wish them happiness with their eternal verities.

Famous Pigs of Literature

OINK. OINK. OINK.

Has anyone ever oinked at you? How did you feel about it? Did you think it was complimentary, even for just one little second? You did not.

We all know that being called a pig is insulting. You can call a woman a mother hen, and a man a bull, but beware calling her a sow or him a swine.

Greedy pig, dirty pig, stupid pig. Pig-headed. Male chauvinist pig. The images are all everyday ones, and all of them cast the pig in a poor light.

Here are three things we all know about pigs: They are greedy, they are dirty, and they oink. But what are we basing this knowledge on? Who among us knows a real, four-legged pig? A few minutes in the agriculture barn at the fall fair, a scattered memory of a pigsty on an uncle's farm, and otherwise the pigs we see are all portioned out and under plastic wrap in the meat department. Most of our knowledge of pigs comes from the famous pigs of literature, and by this I do not mean septuagenarian poets with their hands on the knees of impressionable nineteen-year-olds.

The literary pigs I know best I met through E.B. White, who knew real pigs well, and held them in affectionate regard. They are Wilbur, from *Charlotte's Web*, and the unnamed ailing pig in

White's essay "The Death of a Pig." Wilbur, as any child knows, is a pig being fattened for slaughter, who is saved by the efforts of his friend Charlotte, a spider. She writes "some pig" in her web above his sty, and his resulting fame saves Wilbur from the butcher.

More pigs from popular culture include: The Three Little Pigs, Piglet from Winnie-the-Pooh, Edward Lear's piggy-wig with a ring in the end of his nose, the five little pigs, one of whom goes to market, Snowball, Squealer, and Napoleon from *Animal Farm*, and the pig in the middle, which it is best not to be. Except for the porcine fascists of *Animal Farm* (who are modelled on humans, after all), pigs in literature are mostly a rather appealing lot, not particularly smelly or greedy, and rarely inclined to say oink.

To better understand aversion to pigs, we have to look at religion and anthropology. Pigs are a puzzling animal because they are considered both sacred and unclean. Countless small pigs have participated in purification rites and exorcisms, usually standing in for people as vicarious sacrifices. Attis, Adonis, and Demeter were open to offers of pigs from their worshippers, and the Ceramese of New Guinea believe that pigs are the maiden divinity Hainuwele in disguise—and eat them anyway. But pigs are the animal of choice for driving demons into. Egyptians associated pigs with Seth, the evil god who killed his brother, Osiris. Both Jews and Muslims believe that the pig is unclean and will not eat it. The pigsty is where the prodigal son ends up just before heading home, because he can sink no lower than swine.

That's stating the situation from a human point of view, of course. As is usual in such cases, those who judged pigs as dirty and greedy reveal much of themselves. It is, in general, hard to credit someone else with having motives that are better than our own. For example: some pig behaviour could be called filthy, especially if you, like people in medieval times, had no great fondness for baths.

Pigs will dig a trough with their snouts, urinate into the trough, and wallow in the stinking mud. The reason they do it is no love for stench. Pigs have sensitive skin, and white pigs are especially at risk of sunburns. Pigs sometimes have mites on their skin, which can be smothered by a roll in mud. It is the coolness of what Flanders and Swann's hippopotamus (a close relation of the domestic pig, by the way) calls "glorious mud," that beckons. The urine is just a regrettable means to an end.

People who raise pigs say they are among the cleanest of barnyard animals. All pigs except those who were weaned too young will choose one corner of their quarters as a bathroom. Although pigs like toys, and can be diverted for up to a week by a plastic ball or ribbons tied on a fence, they will not play with any toy that falls by chance into excrement.

My mother's family once raised a runt pig, somewhat like Wilbur in *Charlotte's Web*, except that even when he got big enough to be in the barn, he was still allowed in the house. This was homesteading Alberta, remember, not gentleman-farming Maine. He was a lovely pig, she told us, a good, clean, friendly and affectionate pet, even when he got past the piglet stage. He was so much a favourite of the children that they took him out on family drives in the Model-T, which he dearly loved. On the last day of his life, he rode away to town very happily, with his paws up on the back windowsill and his snout taking in the smells.

Which brings us to the next charge against pigs. "Greedy pigs" is a curious insult to be levelled by the party that plans to kill the pig come fall and eat every bit of it from the snout to the tail. Furthermore, it doesn't show much gratitude for the pig's ability to turn food that people can't eat into food they can. Acorns and peanut husks, bacon grease from the breakfast bacon, excess zucchini, kitchen scraps: pigs can turn all of it back into bacon again. That pigs take an innocent pleasure in making this vast energy conversion is surely not a failing on their part. Still, it's hard to see a creature eat with such gusto and not catch a glimpse of our own greed. How could we recognize gluttony in a pig if we never felt it in ourselves?

Such glimpses of gluttony are getting harder to take here on this hungry planet. Other people are starving, but what can we do about it? It feels better to make gluttony a characteristic of pigs, and have another slice of that ham.

Do pigs oink? They don't in any language other than English. In German they say "quek"; in French they say "groin"; and in Chinese they say "ngert."

People who raise pigs claim a much broader vocabulary for them. "Pigs have many sounds of their own, including the so-called song of love (*chant de coeur*) of the boar that recognizes a sow in heat," writes Dirk van Loon, author of *Small-Scale Pig Raising*. In *Raising Pigs Successfully*, Kathy and Bob Kellogg describe pig talk this way: "There's the shrieking squeal of fear, the 'bark' or 'woof' of alarm or warning, the anguished roars of hungry pigs and the satisfied grunts of happy hogs. But the best of swine language is the happy talk of a sow nursing her litter."

By far the most amusing pig-talk story comes from A.B. Comstock's *A Handbook of Nature Study*. A woman who liked pigs a great deal set to work to learn their language. One day, feeling confident that she could say something in pig, she leaned over the sty, where two sows were eating in companionable silence, and tried out a few phrases. The sows, startled, looked up from the trough and stared at each other for a moment. Then, both assuming that the other had spoken, they started fighting.

What insult was it that the pig-loving woman inadvertently spoke?

I'd like to think it was: "Talk, talk, talk. You eat like a human."

The Crotchety
Old Fudge Recipe

❧

ANY COLD, CLEAR NIGHT IN DECEMBER IS, BY DEFINITION, FUDGE
weather. Waiting for a dry December night sets up a sort of ten-
sion, of course. Suppose the clear night happens in the first week
of the month. Do you make the fudge anyway and try to keep it
until Christmas? How do you hide it from yourself? Or do you
wait, hoping, in the West Coast rainforest, for clear weather closer
to the 25th?

My family's chocolate fudge is one of those obligatory
Christmas recipes we're all stuck with. In an odd way, it's an heir-
loom. When I was a child, I adored it. It was glory among glories,
the most concentrated chocolate taste I knew and as essential as
the bird itself to Christmas dinner. It's true that I didn't have much
to compare it with. No one knew about Belgian bittersweet in
Vancouver's east end in the 1950s. But it is the one sweet treat I
will still "even out" in the pan, the one that obliterates all hope of
satiety and leaves only a longing for more of the same rich, sweet
smoothness in the mouth.

So when fudge weather arrives, I surrender to the force of
habits that stretch over forty years. I check the cupboards, dig out
the recipe—a loose scrap of paper carefully filed somewhere in the
pile that includes Shirley's Cookies, Mia's Granola, Aunt Esther's
Chocolate Cake and Bessie Forster's Carrot-Raisin Bread—and
prepare to do battle.

In my mother's own nest of recipe clippings, a green ring binder held shut by an elastic band, it appears as a yellowed newspaper clipping from the 1940s, titled simply Chocolate Fudge. We called it family fudge. My sister Ann, who found a more reliable recipe years ago, calls it "that damned old thing." The truth is, my family's fudge is a crotchety recipe, utterly intolerant of mistakes and full of non-negotiable demands.

The basic pattern for our recipe is probably nearing a hundred years old, which isn't very old as recipes go. For one thing, it demands a good supply of inexpensive white sugar, and that didn't happen until the 1880s. Fudge is only as old as the first generation of New England women's colleges, where it was first made. In his *Dictionary of American Food and Drink*, John Mariani gives 1896 as the date of the first fudge recipe in print, but writes: "it was commonly associated with college women by that time." Recipes for Vassar fudge and Wellesley fudge occur slightly later.

"Fudge," meaning lies or nonsense, may go back to Captain Fudge, a seventeenth-century English sea captain and a notorious liar. Mariani argues that "fudge" as a name for a candy is more likely derived from "fadge," a word that means to fit pieces together. It may also be derived from fudge as a mild, college-girl's expletive, playfully applied to a frivolous new candy.

Technically, fudge is a candy that is 10 per cent water by weight and has crystals that are 10 microns, or 0.0005 of an inch in size. The small size of the crystals is what makes fudge taste creamy. To turn granulated sugar into chocolate fudge you heat a mixture of milk, sugar, bitter chocolate and corn syrup to the right temperature, a temperature so exact that it has its own name—"soft ball." Sugar syrup hits soft ball between 235° and 240° F (112° and 115° C). Over 240°, it moves through these ascending stages: hard ball, soft crack, and hard crack. As the temperature rises, water is driven off and the syrup becomes more and more saturated. If you don't get it to soft ball, it won't set. If you cook it past soft ball, it will be chalky and dry. The margin for error? One or two per cent spells the difference between success and failure.

Candy thermometers do not give an accurate reading for batches of fudge as small as the one the crotchety fudge recipe makes. That leaves the cold water test: run the water until it is very cold, fill a cereal bowl, then take a spoonful of the bubbling syrup and drop it in the water. If it puddles and pools and balls itself up when you touch it with the spoon, that's soft ball. Then you must immediately and very carefully remove the fudge from the heat.

Cooling the crotchety fudge recipe is just as important as heating it—and just as full of dangers. It should be cooled quickly, preferably outside on the back porch. Here is where fudge weather makes itself felt. If the air is moist the fudge will take up water as it cools and all your care over reaching soft ball goes for naught. There are those who suggest cooking a few degrees past soft ball to compensate for a wet day. I salute their courage.

The crotchety fudge recipe must be handled very carefully at this point. Any one of a number of things can start crystals forming. And crystals that form in a hot liquid are big grainy crystals, not small smooth ones.

Don't jiggle it, for God's sake! Don't stir down any remaining uncooked sugar from the sides and don't poke in a metal spoon for samples because the cold metal can cool the fudge around it sufficiently to start the supersaturated sugar condensing. I prefer to sample by poking in my index finger and scooping up a warm glob of fudge. This method has the side benefit of letting you know if it's cool enough to stir. If you can comfortably leave your finger in there, it's ready.

Beating the fudge is no mean feat and, furthermore, hedged about with potential disaster. When you send a cool, supersaturated solution into steady movement, seed crystals form as the sugar begins to crystallize. But if the fudge moves fast enough, very few molecules can hold on to each seed. Stop stirring to catch your breath and the crystals immediately start enlarging and turning grainy.

When these perils have been braved, we reach the ultimate insult of the crotchety fudge recipe: you can lose it all in the last ten seconds. Judging when to stop stirring is a task for intuition and experience. You may also heed Danish philosopher Piet Hien's advice for making perfect toast: "there's one way to time it / never try to guess / toast it till it smokes / then 20 seconds less." At a moment just before the ribbons of candy start to lose their gloss you must pour the still-liquid fudge into a buttered pan. Stir past that point and it will set in the pan and have to be dug out with spoons.

Why do I continue to subject myself to this ill-tempered recipe at Christmas time? I suspect it's because, after all these years, family fudge appears to me an accurate metaphor for family Christmases. Emotionally supersaturated by the season, we rush around, molecules in rapid motion. Children regularly sugar out, especially when they're overheated, and the rest of us worry that one more bit of careless agitation will send us over the edge. And, like fudge at the moment of setting, family Christmases have their moments of transition. Then you have to intuit a change that has just begun, and to recognize that tradition is sometimes just a name we use for inertia when we feel it in December.

When this story was first published, readers complained because I didn't give the recipe. Here it is. Make it at your own risk.

Chocolate Fudge

3 cups (750 mL) white sugar
2 Tbsp. (30 mL) corn syrup
$^3/_4$ cup (175 mL) milk
2 1-oz. (25-g) squares unsweetened chocolate
$^1/_4$ tsp. (1 mL) salt
1 Tbsp. (15 mL) butter
1 tsp. (5 mL) vanilla
$^1/_2$ cup (125 mL) chopped walnuts

In a medium saucepan, combine the sugar, corn syrup, milk, chocolate, and salt. Cook over low heat, stirring frequently, until the mixture reaches a full boil. Cover the pan and boil 3 minutes to dissolve the crystals. Uncover, cook without stirring until 240°F (115°C) or until the soft ball stage is reached. Remove from the heat without stirring, and add the butter. Let cool and then add the vanilla and walnuts. Beat until creamy (it loses its shine). Pile into a buttered pan or platter, spread with a knife or metal spatula. Score when cold, and refrigerate.

The Flaming
Christmas Pudding

OF ALL THE ODDITIES OF THE CHRISTMAS TABLE, PLUM PUDDING
is surely the oddest.

A dark and leaden hemisphere, exhaling a hot stench of spices
and dried fruits—none of them plums—so rich we can only eat a
spoonful, comes to the table in flames amid general acclamation,
and almost always prompts someone to say "God bless us, every
one."

Yet once the festive meal is over, no one outside Britain will eat
plum pudding again for another year, and few enough there. With
the exception of haggis, itself eaten one day a year by even fewer
people, none of us will eat a single dish from the entire family of
steamed and boiled puddings until Christmas comes around again.

To understand the fix plum pudding finds itself in, imagine
that every other kind of pie has disappeared and the only pie,
served only once a year, is mincemeat. Or that the only cake we
ever make is fruitcake, and all the other cake recipes have fallen out
of use. When Burns called haggis the "chieftain o' the pudding
race," he could not have foreseen a clan with such a bad case of the
dwindles.

Why did all of plum pudding's cousins die out? How did plum
pudding survive the slaughter? And what does it say about us that
we enshrine as the high point of Christmas dinner a dish that we
don't like well enough to eat at any other time?

To begin with the last question, plum pudding shows that we are more subject than we know, both to the powers of storytelling and the need to set fire to something after dinner. The most famous plum pudding in all of fiction is, of course, the "speckled cannon-ball, so hard and firm, blazing in half of half-a-quartern of ignited brandy, and bedight with Christmas holly stuck into the top" carried to the Cratchit's table in the Christmas-present section of *A Christmas Carol.*

A Christmas Carol was and remains enormously popular, with more than two hundred film adaptations, most of them, I suspect, featuring a blazing pudding. On the Prairies in the 1930s, when my parents' Christmas traditions were formed, brandy was medicinal. If there was brandy in the house, it was in a small bottle kept high in the cupboard and doled out by the teaspoon in case of illness and emergency. Pouring it over a pudding and setting fire to it was not in the realm of the possible.

So the first Christmas puddings I remember came with rum sauce and whipped cream, but without benefit of flame. I saved my appetite for the chocolates.

My big sister Ann loves *A Christmas Carol*, especially the movie version with Alistair Sims. Twenty years ago, when she became the maker of the family's Christmas dinner, we started the ritual of heating the brandy, setting the pudding alight and carrying it into the darkened dining room. Now a Christmas without flaming pudding is unthinkable—more unthinkable than it would have been when Dickens wrote the book that has come to define a Victorian Christmas.

In 1843, when *A Christmas Carol* was published, December 25 had been an official national holiday for only nine years, and commercial Christmas cards were a brand new idea. Plum pudding was popular, but by no means fused with the idea of Christmas, and could be eaten year-round. Anthony Trollope's 1858 novel *Doctor Thorne* holds the first mention of plum pudding as "Christmas pudding."

English Christmas feasts had for centuries included a ceremonial dish containing dried fruit. But until the early nineteenth century, it was plum porridge, or frumenty: wheat cooked in milk with sugar, spices, currants and egg yolks. In the nineteenth century, plum pudding took over the ceremonial functions of frumenty, including the custom that everyone in the household must stir it for good luck, and that it must only be stirred in one direction—east to west—to honour the path of the sun, or later, the journey of the Magi.

This was a rise in status for a dish with very humble origins. The Oxford English Dictionary's first definition for pudding is "the stomach or one of the entrails of a pig, sheep or other animal, stuffed with a mixture of minced meat, suet, oatmeal, seasonings, etc., boiled and kept till needed—a sausage." Pudding was made in quantity in the late fall, when animals that weren't going to be fed over winter were slaughtered. As cheap filler, it was served first, with the broth it was boiled in, to blunt—or perhaps bludgeon—the appetite before the meat appeared on the table.

Sixteenth-century England made a lively connection between pudding and guts. Entrails of an animal were called "pudding guts," the "pudding cart" hauled them away from slaughter to the "pudding pit" where they were dumped. A "pudding house" was either a human stomach, in a nod to the ubiquity of pudding, or a place that sold offal.

Then, three hundred years ago, with the invention of the pudding cloth, everything changed. Pudding severed its connection to slaughter and became dessert. The first known recipe for a sweet suet pudding cooked in a bag dates from 1617. It was called Cambridge Pudding and in time, every English college had its own version. Sweet pudding, served after dinner, was so universal that "pudding" became British for dessert. As Alan Davidson writes in *The Oxford Companion to Food*, "what's for pud', mum?" is "a question to which the answer might be 'ice cream' or 'an apple'."

The United Farm Women of Alberta's cookbook that my Aunt Harriet gave my mother in 1946 has thirty recipes for steamed puddings, including: ginger pudding, California pudding, carrot pudding, economical pudding, and several versions of plum pudding and Christmas pudding. By that time, the pudding cloth had been superceded by the even more convenient pudding basin, a bowl with a rim around which sealing paper could be tied. Pudding-bowl puddings are always steamed, with the hot water coming halfway up the sides of the bowl.

Then puddings died out, almost entirely.

Stodge may be out of fashion, and suet has developed an unhappy reputation for clogging arteries. But the real reason why no one throws together a steamed pudding for a casual dessert these days is that a steamed pudding demands a minimum of two and a half hours of cooking time, and larger ones cook for six hours or more.

Alone of all its kin, plum pudding survives because it's "plum." This has less to do with prunes than it does with the Medieval English habit of calling all dried fruit, including raisins, "plums." In a time of comparatively little sugar, the sweetness, along with the chewy texture, of dried fruits made them exciting to eat. "Plum" came to mean the best of things—a meaning we keep in phrases like "a plum job." For a time, "a plum" stood for 100,000 pounds sterling, and also for the man who owned such a magnificent sum.

Jack Horner's plum was probably a raisin. But another explanation of the nursery rhyme throws light on how far from a prune a plum might stray.

In this story, Jack, steward to the Abbot of Glastonbury, was charged with delivering the deeds to the monastery's properties to Henry VIII, when Henry dissolved the Church's holdings. For safety, the deeds were concealed in a pastry. On his way to the royal court, Jack is supposed to have lifted the crust and pulled out the deed to the Manor of Wells—a plum indeed—and one that was occupied by his descendants for several centuries.

The pudding we still eat is the best pudding, rich with raisins, currants, candied peel, eggs, almonds, spices and alcohol, lightened a little with flour and grated carrot. It is also a very good thing to set fire to after dinner.

In the northern hemisphere, we need an act of sympathetic magic to bring back the sun. Writing of Christmas pudding, Alan Davidson notes that the Celtic winter solstice fire festival is "still frankly celebrated in the Orkneys with the rite of Up Helly A, when a ship is burnt." A pudding may not have the gravitas of a boat, but for tabletop flames, it's hard to beat. Anything that weighs so much more than you thought it would when you picked it up demands respect, and suggests other spherical weighty objects, like planets. Surprisingly, Christmas pudding has not always been the top choice of ceremonial fire, even when it was available. I have a friend whose family Christmas dinner featured a flaming duck, an unintentional echo of colonial American tables at which the turkey was set ablaze.

Sometimes it was the mince pies that ignited—not always to approval. In *The Christmas Cook: Three Centuries of American Yuletide Sweets*, food historian William Woys Weaver quotes prolific cookbook author Miss Eliza Leslie, writing in 1857: "The foolish custom of setting the pies on fire after they come to the table and causing a blue blaze to issue from the liquor that is in them, is now obsolete, and considered ungenteel and tavern-like. If this practice originated in a polite desire to *frighten the ladies*, its purpose is already a failure, for the ladies are not frightened; that is, not really."

On the other hand, perhaps the purpose was to light a flame for the new year, in which case it succeeded. May your pudding burn bright.

This is the pudding recipe my sister Ann has been making for years, a borrowing from her friend Jean. The grated vegetables make it lighter than most. The "deluxe fruit cake mix" called for in the recipe is a standard mix of candied fruit and peel that grocers stock in time for Christmas cakes and puddings.

Favourite Christmas Pudding

1 cup (250 mL) bread crumbs
²/₃ cup (150 mL) raisins
1 cup (250 mL) deluxe fruit cake mix
²/₃ cup (150 mL) currants
1 cup (250 mL) pastry flour
³/₄ tsp. (4 mL) baking powder
³/₄ tsp. (4 mL) baking soda
1 tsp. (5 mL) salt
1 tsp. (5 mL) cinnamon
¹/₄ tsp. (1 mL) each of nutmeg, cloves, ginger, allspice
²/₃ cup (150 mL) finely chopped vegetarian or beef suet
²/₃ cup (150 mL) grated apple
²/₃ cup (150 mL) grated potato
²/₃ cup (150 mL) grated carrot
2 eggs
¹/₂ cup (125 mL) liquid honey
¹/₄ cup (50 mL) brandy for flaming

In a large bowl, combine the bread crumbs and fruit.

Sift the flour once, measure, add the baking powder, soda, salt, and spices, and re-sift over the fruit mixture. Mix well, coating the fruit with the flour.

Add the suet, apple, potato, and carrot to the fruit mixture.

Beat the eggs until thick and light, and then add the honey. Add the egg mixture to the fruit mix. Blend thoroughly.

Spoon into a well-greased 30-oz. (800-mL) pudding bowl. Cover the top with aluminum foil, pleating the foil to allow the pudding to expand. (The pudding mixture will come to the top of the bowl.) Tie the foil into place with twine.

Steam on a rack in a pot of gently boiling water for two and a half hours. Remove from the heat and let cool. Remove from the pudding bowl. Wrap the pudding in plastic wrap and then in foil. Store in the refrigerator or freezer.

To serve: defrost the frozen pudding. Remove the plastic wrap.

Re-wrap the pudding in foil. Reheat in a 325°F (160°C) oven for 30 minutes. Place on a heat-proof platter and garnish with holly. In small saucepan, warm the brandy, pour over the pudding, and ignite. A long match keeps your hands a comfortable distance from the flames.

Once the flames die out—they should burn for about a minute—serve with Rum Sauce (see below) and whipped cream.

Makes 10 to 12 servings.

This sauce can be made a day ahead and stored in a sealed container in the fridge. Warm it briefly in the microwave before serving. If you love rum, use Demerara for its deep, dark taste. If you're iffy on the taste of rum, start with two tablespoons and taste your way up.

Rum Sauce

1 cup (250 mL) sugar
1 Tbsp. (15 mL) cornstarch
2 Tbsp. (30 mL) butter
1 cup (250 mL) boiling water
1/4 cup (50 mL) amber rum

In a medium saucepan, mix the sugar and cornstarch. Add the butter and boiling water. Bring to a boil and cook until thickened, about 3 minutes. Remove from the heat and cool to room temperature. Stir in the rum.

Makes 1³/4 cups (425 mL).

Wood Stove

ONE SUMMER I SPENT A WEEK ON AN ISLAND TOO SPARSELY populated to support a store, perfectly content cooking on a wood stove in a cabin with no electricity and no running water. I came back half convinced that our kitchens don't ask too much of us, but too little.

That doesn't mean I want primitive fixtures in my city kitchen. (A tiger's love for her kittens pales beside my love for my dishwasher.) But once in a while, I like to reconnect with fire. For if cooking is a matter of reading labels and pushing buttons, then how important can eating be? If cooking means evoking the fire god and courting him through the tempestuous drama of roasting a chicken, then what comes to the table is an offering, and thanksgivings are due if it isn't burnt.

For visitors, the island is a place of gently enforced inactivity. People swim in the lake, or row out on the battered rowboat to see the family of loons at the other end. Or they go for walks along the path by the water, or through the fields that a big, hard-working Swede homesteaded in the 1930s. He planted orchards and fruit and vegetables, and built rock retaining walls around parts of the lake, and canned and ate his horse Lindy after she accidentally hung herself in one of the apple trees.

Six people bought the land in the early 1970s and built some cabins. In mid-July, the family that has claim to the old farmhouse was there, a couple and two children. So was the property's caretaker, who farms a little garlic and keeps a vegetable garden. He lives year-round in a cabin close to the old homestead. His son, a four-year-old wild man with hair to mid-back, like his father's, and a grubby fist forever brushing it from his face, was one reason I wanted to make cookies. The boy had a Popeye doll, and a beaten-up plush parrot. When I held the parrot on Popeye's shoulder and croaked "pieces of eight, pieces of eight" at him, he looked at the parrot with desperate regret, and said, "I don't have those." I wanted more access to the world of a four-year-old. He had a sweet tooth, and I am not above bribery.

Going to the island means going back to turn-of-the-century technology, to wood stoves and kerosene lanterns. Our friend Jerome, known to his partners as Mr. Crisp for his fastidious ways, has a propane fridge that miraculously makes ice cubes. Small quantities of ice cubes, to be sure, but enough to clink in a glass at the end of a hard day's basking on the rocks and cooling off in the lake.

I brought to the island olive oil, basil and thyme from my garden, the pasta shells I like for pasta salad, sun-dried tomatoes, artichokes, olives, sweet onions, Belgian chocolate, and, on impulse, a little jug of real maple syrup. Blueberries, lots of lemons, oranges, apples, baking soda and powder. Smoked salmon. Sausage and cheese. A dozen beer, a bottle of Scotch. A roasting chicken, frozen solid, bought from the last big supermarket on the route. The dense, heavy sunflower-seed bread from the bakery down the street. And one litre of milk. If we hadn't had to carry the food on a trail that climbed from the ocean, then dipped into the lake, there would have been more milk.

As for the rationale behind the rest of the shopping list, I reasoned that we could always go to the next big island for staples. But we'd have to come right back to civilization before we found a store selling Belgian chocolate and sun-dried tomatoes.

I can swim and read and lie in the sun only for so long. I take a certain pleasure in hacking back salal so that a walk along the path after a rain doesn't soak the shins, but that's the sort of thing I want to do for only twenty minutes at a time, to clear my head. I had endless time for cooking. And because there was no store, I was blessed by limits. Except for the beans and beets, all coming ripe at once in the caretaker's garden, the materials were finite. What we had was what we were going to eat, so I was free to concentrate on the food at hand.

The first meals were simple, with a minimum of cooking: smoked salmon and cream cheese on slices of sunflower bread, with fresh thyme, a drop of lemon, a little black pepper and a slice of sweet onion. Then a green salad with olives and artichokes for heft, and sun-dried tomatoes for salty, concentrated flavour. Then fruit and chocolate for dessert.

Sometime in the two years since Jerome had last stayed at the cabin, someone had borrowed the sugar. No one wanted sugar in coffee or on cereal or fruit. But once we lit the wood stove, I wanted to bake. We had fresh flour. There was a copy of the aptly named *Joy of Cooking* on the shelf, and two flour-company cookbooks, the kind that are a monument to the marriage of commerce and cooking. My mother used to say: "They want to sell more flour, so everything in there is guaranteed to work," and she was right.

We first lit the oven to bake the chicken. And if the oven was on for chicken, there was no reason, apart from the sugar shortage, not to bake cookies. I studied *Joy of Cooking*, and with the help of the sugar substitution chart, made thin, crisp, elegantly coffee-coloured maple chocolate chip cookies, the chips cut from the block of Belgian chocolate. They tasted magnificent. The chicken roasted to red-brown, crisp on the skin and juicy inside. I was in love.

I had never been in charge of a wood stove before. When I was a child, and saw them in my prairie aunts' kitchens, they frightened me. You would burn if you brushed against one, which was not true of the electric stove at home. To me, wood stoves were just one more proof that the country is full of dangerous unknowns, and the city is safe. Later I stayed in cabins with wood stoves, but I was unsure of my skills. Besides, there was always someone there first, already weaving the dance of fire. Poke the fire, or add a stick of wood, and you would only throw them off their game.

My knowledge of fire is far from perfect. But I can light one, and keep it going, and modulate its temperature. As days went by, I studied the science of the damper, opening and closing it to feed air to my fire or starve it. I leapt to the pleasant challenge, at the end of the baking time, of stirring up the coals just enough to keep the oven heat constant, without having to add more wood. I was playing with fire, a game made all the more involving because of the stove's defects. Rust had loosened the oven handle and opened a hole in the oven wall above the door, and another between the oven and the top of the firebox. When the fire was too hot, you could see orange flames rush over the oven roof. The required adjustments were minute but constant.

I never got around to learning to tell the temperature by the number of seconds I could keep my hand in the hot oven. I'm told that's the sign of a wood-stove master. But I cooked, using a far bigger chunk of attention and skill than it ever takes to set a number on a dial. On the last afternoon, I made cinnamon buns. I had time to nurse the dough, and the classic place to let it rise: the shelf over the stove. When I lifted the bread bowl to put it in place, I felt centuries of cooks with bread bowls stretch into the past behind me.

I put the buns in to bake after dinner, while we did the dishes. We waited for them on the deck, drinking plum wine that Jerome had made seven summers before. Six rainy winters at the back of a kitchen cupboard can have good effects or ill. This wine was as clear and as rarefied as good slivovitz, the dry, slightly bitter, plum brandy.

The oven was warm and glowing. Too warm, I realized, when I saw through the hole over the handle of the oven door a stream of molten air, quick with sparks, flowing over the oven roof. I put a few light pan lids in place to protect the buns, but it singed the top of some of them. By the time the dough was baked, the surfaces that weren't under the lids were charred.

From Jerome's deck, you can see lake through the trees, and hear loons on the lake. We drank plum wine and ate cinnamon buns brushed by fire and spread with the last of the butter. While we ate, the bats came out to trace the rapid kiss of their black shapes on the sky.

I have never since found myself with maple syrup, a need to make cook-
ies, and no sugar, but I have made these cookies again. They're perfect
cookies to make on a whim, a small batch that mixes up in the time it
takes the oven to heat, and irresistible while they're still warm. I make
them small, so they have plenty of room to spread on the cookie sheet.

Maple Syrup Chocolate Chip Cookies

$^1/_2$ cup (125 mL) very soft butter
$^1/_2$ cup (125 mL) maple syrup
1 egg
$^1/_2$ tsp. (2 mL) vanilla
1 cup (250 mL) flour
$^1/_2$ tsp. (2 mL) baking soda
$^1/_2$ cup (125 mL) coarsely chopped Belgian semi-sweet chocolate

Preheat the oven to 350°F (180°C).

In a medium mixing bowl, beat the butter and syrup together with an electric mixer until smooth. Add the egg and vanilla and beat until well mixed. Add the flour, baking soda, salt, and chocolate.

Using a teaspoon, drop the dough onto a greased baking sheet. Bake for 12 minutes, or until the edges are browned.

Makes $2^1/_2$ dozen cookies.

Rye

I GREW UP IN A HOUSE RULED BY TWO ANTAGONISTIC SPIRITS: the Women's Christian Temperance Union and rye whisky.

My mother didn't touch a drop. Whenever the subject of drinking came up she claimed to be president of the WCTU. Officially, she was working on us all to take the pledge. Unofficially, she was willing to tolerate my father's modest consumption of beer in the summer and rye in the winter.

Drinking was something men did that women wished they wouldn't. The men drank rye because they were prairie boys transplanted to the West Coast by the Depression and the Second World War. I grew up believing that all men liked rye, and all women loathed it.

At Christmas parties the women sat upstairs in the living room and drank tea. The men went to the basement to look at whatever home improvement was underway and to drink. The mothers had better food, but the fathers smelled of illicit excitement and rye. They drank ginger ale or 7-Up mixed with rye, or, occasionally, Coke with Lamb's Navy Rum. You could drink all the soft drinks you wanted and the men, co-conspirators, never told you to stop. Besides, there was an outside chance that someone would bring a bottle to add to our stocks of V.O. It was an even more outside chance that the bottle would be Seagram's Crown Royal, which came in a purple and gold drawstring bag—perfect for marbles.

But lightning does strike, and a child in the right place at the right time could score big. The danger of hanging out with the dads was that one of them might turn toward you and exhale a jovial blast of wet, fermented rye-stink. Of all the terrible ways that adults smelled, rye was surely the worst. The arms of temperance never looked more welcoming.

I think of this early exposure to Calvinism and second-hand rye as a sort of national oscillation expressed in microcosm—the Scots and Irish may rave about their whiskies and the French about their wines, but Canadians are not really sure we approve of our national drink. Some friends of mine put together a Scotch club a few years ago and spent a number of evenings tasting all the single-malt Scotch whiskies they could lay their hands on. Sampling every available rye wouldn't occur to them.

I shouldn't really be calling it rye, of course. What comes inside the purple velvet bag is Canadian whisky, "the classic mixable whisky" as Rosalind Cooper's *Spirits and Liqueurs* tactfully puts it, a blend of as many as seventy different whiskies, 90 per cent of it highly distilled neutral spirits—colourless, flavourless alcohol.

Hiram Walker, an American, launched the first identifiable brand of Canadian whisky—Canadian Club—largely by accident. Walker had a dry goods store in Detroit that included a liquor department. In 1856, with an eye to laxer liquor laws and lower Canadian land prices, he bought 468 acres of land just east of Windsor, and built a flour mill, distillery, hog farm, and, eventually, a company town.

Milling, distilling, and livestock have always gone together. Farmers bring the grain, the miller grinds it, and cash-poor farmers pay for his services in grain. If the miller has a still, he can make whisky from the extra grain and feed the used mash to his hogs.

In nineteenth-century Canada, millers had a lot of rye. Among the cereals, rye has a reputation as a rank weed that will grow in worse soils and colder climates than more highly prized grains. For the new settlers who watched their wheat succumb to cold and disease, rye was a dependable crop.

Distillers of the time smoothed their whisky through double-distillation, charcoal leaching, or aging. Walker put his rye mash, mixed with corn, through a long, intense distillation process, then blended the whisky with colourless, flavourless, neutral spirits. What you got was a lighter, smoother, crisper spirit with some of what *World Guide to Whisky* author Michael Jackson calls "the spicy, bitter-sweet character of rye." But not too much: in Canadian whisky there can be as little as 3 per cent straight rye whisky, more often 4 or 5 per cent. The main ingredient in the mash is generally corn.

At a time when most distillers sold their whisky in unmarked barrels, Walker bottled his whisky and labelled it Walker's Club Whisky. He also labelled his barrels. Walker's Club Whisky was "meant to be a sophisticated whisky for clubmen . . . a whisky for gentlemen, not for rednecks," Jackson writes.

In 1880, American distillers petitioned Washington for regulations that would require importers to state the country of origin on imported liquor. Hiram Walker, who continued to live in Detroit, complied, and Canadian Club was born.

Straight rye whisky, now defined as having at least 51 per cent rye cereal, never achieved the popularity of blended ryes, and Canadian distillers have not tried to win a place for it. Blended Canadian whisky has a slightly less ironclad legal description. Here it is, from U.S. regulations: "Canadian rye whisky shall be whisky distilled in Canada, and shall possess the aroma, taste and character generally attributable to Canadian whisky."

It's almost poetic, isn't it? The Canadian water of life: named for a grain that adapts well to cold weather, blended from a multitude of sources, and defined by consensus. If it's not American or British, it's Canadian. If it has the qualities "generally attributable" to Canadian whisky, then it's Canadian whisky. Perhaps it is characteristic of us that we've never taken to it entirely.

Temperance has been around in Canada almost as long as anyone has been here distilling whisky. According to William Rannie in *Canadian Whisky: the product and the industry*, the first commercial still devoted to whisky was probably John Molson's, opened in 1799 at L'Assomption, Québec. The first temperance society was formed at West River, Pictou County, Nova Scotia, in 1827—less than 30 years later. By the late nineteenth century, prohibition was gathering steam. Under the 1878 Canada Temperance Act, people could vote to go dry region by region. Saskatchewan embraced prohibition in 1915, Alberta in 1916, B.C. in 1917. In 1918, national prohibition was declared, to extend for a period of one year after the end of the First World War.

There were loopholes, of course. In Ontario, you could get a quart of whisky for medicinal purposes, with a prescription. The medicinal qualities of whisky suddenly received a lot more attention. "It is necessary to go to a drug store and lean up against the counter and make a gurgling sigh like apoplexy," Stephen Leacock wrote. "One often sees these apoplexy cases lined up four deep."

Rye found its biggest popularity following the repeal of Prohibition in the U.S. when foresighted men like Sam Bronfman, founder of the Seagram empire, sent stocks of aged whisky to a nation that hadn't seen anything like it in years.

Lately rye has slipped in popularity, pushed out by lighter drinks such as white rum, vodka, and tequila. I bought a mickey of Canadian Club recently—if memory serves, the first I've ever bought. The bite at the back of the throat isn't as fierce as I remember it from tasting my father's drinks. But it brought with it a memory of jovial men coming up the basement stairs. There was always a moment of chill when they hit the living room, reeking of rye. The chill never lasted. It was Christmas and they were, as I said, jovial men. We ate cheese and cold meats, Ritz crackers with cheddar cheese, celery sticks filled with Cheez Whiz, Christmas cake, and Christmas cookies. And teatotallers and drinkers alike, we drank quantities of tea, in air lightly scented by rye.

HUNGRY QUESTIONS

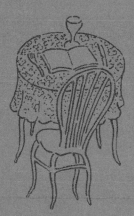

How Marilyn Monroe
Is Like a Grilled Artichoke

❦

IN 1948, NORMA JEAN BAKER REIGNED AS THE QUEEN OF THE FIRST Castroville, California, Artichoke Festival. This is the only link I know of between the blond bombshell and the vegetable that looks like a hand grenade, and on the surface it seems like a tenuous one.

According to *The Sensuous Artichoke*, by brother and sister Angelo-Charles and Catherine A. Castelli, that's not so. In what is surely the world's most exhaustive work on the biology, chemistry, history, lore, and world distribution of the artichoke, Angelo-Charles Castelli, a retired publicist who spent part of his career promoting Cynar, an Italian artichoke liqueur, writes that far from being just another pretty young girl in a marriage of convenience with a vegetable, "Marilyn embodied the qualities of the artichoke and captured the essence of the artichoke in her body movements and demeanor."

Okay, I'll admit it's a stretch. Marilyn was a creature of soft and willing flesh, the essence of accessibility. The artichoke, by contrast, is an object lesson in defence. We eat the bases of the leaves and the pad of the artichoke, the fleshy receptacle that anchors the flower petals. To reach the tender heart, you have to remove the tough outer leaves, which sometimes have spines on the ends. Inside the leaves, the immature flower petals create another line of defence. "Choke" is an apt term for these densely packed threads.

They go everywhere, stick to everything, and are hugely irritating to the throat if accidentally eaten. (Choking is not part of the original meaning of "artichoke." The word comes from the Arabic *al-kharshof,* which entered English as *artechock,* meaning "the artichoke," with no distress implied. The change to "choke" came later.)

Even more disconcerting is the vegetable's ability to create an insane amount of waste. The leaves and choke are so tightly packed that freeing the heart sets off a sort of slow-motion explosion. The initial trimmings from six artichokes—remove the stalks, strip off the outer leaves, and slice a third of the remaining leaves off the top, being sure to rub every cut surface with a slice of lemon—fills a plastic grocery bag. Remove the choke and the inner circle of leaves that enclose it and you create another pile of discards. When the artichoke finally reaches the table, the third and final pile of debris manages to be somehow larger than the artichoke before it was eaten. *New York Times* food writer Amanda Hesser recommends that you keep corn on the cob in mind as you trim. After all, no one minds shucking corn, or throwing away the cobs.

And there are at least two good reasons why we might begin to ask: How can we make an artichoke be more like Marilyn Monroe?

Anything that tastes as good as a fresh artichoke ought to be made more accessible. Besides, artichokes are full of health-promoting phyto-chemicals. If we could just cozy up to them, we'd be doing ourselves a favour.

In May 2002, for example, *Prevention* magazine reported on a German study in which researchers gave 143 patients with elevated total cholesterol (more than 280) 1800 milligrams of dry artichoke extract or a dummy pill daily for six weeks. By the end of the study, those who took the artichoke extract lowered their cholesterol by an average of 18 per cent, while the placebo group's cholesterol dropped by only about 8 per cent. In addition, the patients who took the artichoke extract improved their ratios of protective HDL cholesterol to "bad" LDL cholesterol, and the improvement was achieved without side effects.

The active ingredient is a chemical called cynarin, which increases the production of bile in the liver and boosts the flow of bile from the gallbladder. Bile plays a key role in removing excess cholesterol from the body. Media response to the news on the health-giving powers of artichokes has been muted, especially in comparison to the commotion over broccoli and oat bran. Nutritionists have not been stepping up to point out that if artichoke essence takes cholesterol out of the blood and aids liver functioning, frequent moderate amounts of the whole food might help keep cholesterol low and the liver healthy to begin with.

I suspect it's the artichoke's image of fussiness that keeps us from embracing it. Even without its defences, a steamed artichoke evokes a very different sensibility from, say, Lorelei Lee, the character Marilyn plays in *Gentlemen Prefer Blondes*. Served one to a person, with a sauce for dipping and a bowl for the discarded leaves, this is a thinner, finer approach to bodily pleasures, one that might even be called dry.

In Jane Grigson's *Vegetable Book*, the eminent British food writer calls artichokes eaten in this way "the vegetable expression of . . . increasing delight by anticipation and crescendo," with "no place in the troll's world of instant gratification," and speculates that this might be the source of its aphrodisiac reputation. It's a widely shared belief, this idea that the artichoke's erotic powers lie in the ritual of scraping away the flesh of the leaves with the teeth, of slowly undressing the artichoke down to its heart. How arousing you find it depends, I suspect, on your patience with striptease.

If that were all that artichokes have to offer, hungry lovers might be inclined to seek something with less foreplay and more resolution. But the artichoke, as we already know, contains powerful phyto-chemicals. In Catherine de Medici's day, a young woman who valued her reputation would never eat an artichoke in public because every authority from Pliny on knew that artichokes provoked lust, especially when cooked in wine. Catherine, who is credited with bringing artichokes from Italy to the French court, was inordinately fond of them. In *Food*, the late Waverley Root, dean of American food writers, tells us that Catherine's public indulgence in artichokes provoked a shocked elderly woman of the time to write, "If one of us had eaten artichokes we would have been pointed out in the street. Today young women are more forward than pages at the court." In fact, Catherine ate so many at a wedding feast in 1575 that she made herself ill—which suggests that she was not scraping one leaf at a time over her teeth in an orgy of delayed gratification.

My theory is that the way to make artichokes more like Marilyn Monroe is to abandon the fussy ritual of serving whole steamed artichokes and, instead, grill them. Trim them, steam them until tender to the point of a knife, cut them in half vertically, clean out the chokes, then marinate them for three hours or more in olive oil, lemon juice, garlic, and shallots. Just before dinner, grill them for five minutes on each side. The fire caramelizes the abundant sugars in the artichoke, and charring adds its own dark layer of taste. If you want to, you can pull away and eat the remaining leaves slowly. Or you can come at the bottom from the bottom, and consume it in three or four sweet earthy bites.

A globe artichoke is never more beautiful than when you cut it in half to reveal a purple flower enclosed by green petals. That's a sight for the cook's eyes alone, since the easiest way to remove the choke is to first grasp the purple petals and pull them out.

Grilled Artichokes

4 large globe artichokes
$\frac{1}{2}$ cup (125 mL) olive oil
$\frac{1}{4}$ cup (50 mL) freshly squeezed lemon juice
2 cloves garlic, minced
1 shallot, minced
salt and freshly ground black pepper

Bend back the outer petals of artichokes until they snap off easily near the base. Cut off the stems and top one-third of the artichokes. Steam over boiling water for about 25 minutes, checking after 20 minutes. They are cooked when the bottom yields to a knifepoint but is not mushy.

Cut the cooked artichokes in half, lengthwise. When they've cooled enough to handle, remove the "chokes"—the hairy fibres just above the heart.

In a small bowl, whisk together the olive oil, lemon juice, garlic, shallot, salt and pepper. Pour the marinade over the artichokes and set aside for at least three hours.

Drain the artichokes and cook over a hot grill for 5 minutes on each side.

Makes 4 appetizer servings.

Mangoes and Sticky Rice

I DON'T REMEMBER NOW IF I FIRST ATE MANGOES AND STICKY rice on the day we followed a monk off the Chao Phya river ferry into a meditation compound and were invited to spend a night in a coffin by the river. It could just as easily have been the day we found a distressed kingfisher chick in an abandoned temple and brought him home to an infancy of minced raw fish and a nest of shredded newspaper. Every day in Bangkok was dramatic, and it's hard to keep them straight.

We were staying with a distant connection—my husband's youngest brother's friend's oldest brother Rick and his wife Flo. Flo was weeks away from delivering her first child and doubly food-obsessed, being both pregnant and Singaporean. One morning after breakfast she announced her plans to make a Thai specialty, the defining dish of Bangkok in the spring: mangoes and sticky rice. It was going to be a big undertaking, requiring special rice, a long period of soaking, delicate kitchen manoeuvres and fully ripe mangoes.

I wasn't looking forward to it. The air was so hot and humid that the word "sticky" carried unappetizing overtones. I imagined white rice for dessert and wished she would save herself the trouble. But that was before I tasted it. Flo emerged from doing battle with the kitchen gods carrying a platter heaped with rice covered with sliced mangoes. When she set it down on the table, it looked like far too much. It wasn't.

What I had failed to imagine is how the rice, at body temperature, would be robed in coconut milk, how it would be both sweet and salty, how the coconut milk would echo the hints of coconut in the mangoes, and how pleasing it would be to feel the cool slip of a mango slice against the firm, warm rice.

Since that evening I've come to believe that mangoes and sticky rice is not just arguably the best dessert ever to come out of Asia, but one of the best summertime desserts in existence. It's as comforting as rice pudding, as erotic as ripe fruit. Any sweet-acid fruit at its peak will work in place of the mangoes: strawberries that haven't travelled, ripe peaches, nectarines, plums, raspberries.

If you're Thai, and need your sticky rice made with every shiny grain of rice separate and, furthermore, lined up in the same direction, it takes some delicate handling. For less demanding cooks, making mangoes and sticky rice is easier and less time-consuming than making a fruit crisp.

The list of virtues continues: it's elegant enough for a dinner party and homey enough to eat for breakfast, well suited for cottage cooking because, apart from the fruit, all of the ingredients are shelf-stable, and it's inexpensive. In Vancouver you can buy two kilograms (five pounds) of top-quality sticky rice for about three dollars.

So why isn't mangoes and sticky rice already a North American summer staple? I think it's partly because "sticky rice" sounds like an unpromising dessert, and partly because it demands a different cooking method from most of the rice we eat.

All rice fits on a continuum from waxy to non-waxy, depending on the relative balance between amylose and amylopectin, two starches in the rice grain. Thai sticky rice is about as low amylose, and therefore as waxy, as rice gets. This bit of chemistry changes everything, from the colour of the raw rice, which is opaque rather than translucent, to the texture when it's cooked, the cooking method, and the taste.

Sticky rice needs to be soaked in cold water for at least three hours at room temperature before it's cooked. In the fridge, it can soak for as long as 12 hours. Then the rice is steamed, over—but not touching—boiling water. You can, if you like, buy a special conical basket and small metal pot for cooking sticky rice. It's easy enough to find in Asian specialty stores, and available by mail order. A Seattle company specializing in Thai food, <ImportFood.com> will sell you a steamer for about US$10 and a basket for US$5.

You can also use a Chinese bamboo steamer with big slats, and line the bottom with cheesecloth or banana leaves (available in Asian markets). As Naomi Duguid, a Toronto-based cookbook author, who, with husband Jeffrey Alford, wrote the authoritative book *Seductions of Rice,* points out, "With a lot of people to feed, you can stack the bamboo steamers."

Montri Rattanaraj, whose Montri Thai Restaurant in Vancouver is one of the few restaurants that serves mangoes and sticky rice in season, puts the soaked rice in the centre of a two-foot square of cloth, folds the corners in to cover it and keep the condensation out, and steams it in a flat metal steamer.

Rattanaraj recommends Rose brand Pin Kiew glutinous rice, which comes from a famous district outside the northern Thai city of Chiang Mai called San Ba Tong. "It has to be from there," he says. "It's a special growing area, like Bing cherries from the Okanagan."

When he was 17, on his first visit to Bangkok, his cousin took him to a renowned sticky rice stall in a food market below New Road, where people lined up all day to buy the most perfect sticky rice available. "I don't know what their secret was," he says. "It might have been a special technique."

In general, the techniques for making coconut sticky rice are well known to Thai cooks. You must stir only in one direction. You must use only a wooden spoon. Metal would be too harsh. And you must not break the grains.

Once you have the right rice and the right cooking method, the last critical detail is the proportion of salt, sugar, and coconut milk to rice. The good news here is that it's hard to be wrong, since much depends on your taste. Nathan Hyam, a Vancouver chef and author of *New Thai Cuisine*, says: "Pretty much every dish has a hundred variations. It depends on where you're from, and what your parents cooked like."

Set the rice to soak before you go to work and it will be ready to cook when you get home. Put it on to steam as you make dinner—35 minutes should be plenty of time—and add the cooked, sweetened coconut milk just as you sit down to eat. There's nothing more to do but slice the fruit and observe the results.

"When I watch people have their first experience of it, there's perhaps a slight caution—white rice for dessert?—then this amazed surprise spreads over their face," Naomi Duguid says. "Then they help themselves to more. You need to make a big platter, and lots of it."

The hardest thing about making this recipe is remembering to set the rice aside to soak early enough. Otherwise it's as easy a dessert as you can make. Try it when local strawberries are in season.

Mangoes and Sticky Rice

1^1/2 cups (375 mL) Thai glutinous rice
1 14-oz (398-mL) can coconut milk
^{1}/2 cup (125 mL) sugar
1 tsp. (5 mL) salt
6 ripe mangoes, peeled, seeded, and sliced

Place the rice in a bowl and cover with cold water. Soak for at least 3 hours at room temperature or, refrigerated, overnight. Drain and rinse thoroughly. Place in a bamboo steamer lined with cheesecloth or banana leaves.

In a wok, bring 2 inches (5 cm) water to a rolling boil. Put the lid on the bamboo steamer and place in the wok. Reduce heat to medium-high and maintain a steady flow of steam. Steam the rice for 35 to 45 minutes, adding water to the saucepan as needed. The rice is cooked when it swells and glistens and is sticky enough to be squeezed into lumps.

While the rice is steaming, stir the coconut milk, sugar, and salt together in a saucepan. Cook, stirring, over medium heat until the sugar dissolves. Set aside.

Place the cooked rice in a bowl and pour the coconut milk mixture over it. Cover the rice and set aside until liquid is absorbed, about 1 hour.

Mound the hot sweetened rice on a serving platter and smooth the surface. Allow to cool to room temperature. Surround the rice with the sliced mangoes and serve.

Serves 4.

Figs: An Appreciation

"TO EAT FIGS OFF THE TREE IN THE VERY EARLY MORNING, WHEN they have barely been touched by the sun, is one of the exquisite pleasures of the Mediterranean," eminent British food writer Elizabeth David wrote, and I believe her.

Even when you buy them in the market, when they have spent a day at the packer's in Fresno, California, made a trip up the coast, and passed another day in a Lower Mainland wholesaler's warehouse, fresh figs are an exquisite pleasure.

Drab on the outside, they are voluptuous within. Yellow-green Kadotas run with a juice so thick it's like syrup. Fresh figs are a classic Italian appetizer, especially when wrapped with a slice of prosciutto. They're a revelation in an arugula salad, and a perfect miniature meal on their own—a plate of figs eaten outside in late summer sunshine.

So why does 98 per cent of the California fig crop end up dried, while only two per cent remains for the fresh and canned market? Why does the height of fig season come and go from our local markets in a week or two, while figs hang in orchards, ready for picking?

Figs are tender and easily bruised. They never get sweet if they're picked too green, and they suffer on the road if they aren't. So most fresh figs are eaten in the warm, dry climates where they grow, and there's the end of it.

But tomatoes and strawberries are as fragile and as poor in quality when picked underripe, yet an entire industry exists to breed roadworthy, albeit insipid, specimens and ship them to us for as long as the season lasts.

Part of our indifference to fresh figs is a sad confusion between fresh figs and dried. We encourage this confusion by using the same word for both, which makes as much culinary sense as having one word for both grapes and raisins.

"Fig," furthermore, is no compliment to the fruit. When Edward Lear's Jumblies ("Their heads are green and their hands are blue, / And they went to sea in a Sieve,") pushed off amid warnings of catastrophe, they shouted back to the naysayers on the shore: "Our Sieve ain't big, / But we don't care a button! we don't care a fig! / In a Sieve we'll go to sea." We all know that what they meant is that they didn't care at all. As the *Oxford English Dictionary* tells us, a fig "is a type of anything small, valueless or contemptible."

Those of us who love fresh figs also know that the fruit the Jumblies referred to had to be dried figs, which, at their worst, somewhat resemble buttons in texture, if not taste.

Fresh figs are something completely different. Cut open a fresh fig and what falls back from the knife is a secret chamber lined with flowers. The fig's coat can be black, brown, red, green, yellow-green, purple, or white, the skin is soft and smooth, the shape simple and modest. Inside, the colour is almost always some shade of pink, from pale to intense. The form is a botanical marvel calling out for Judy Chicago or Georgia O'Keeffe.

Every fig we eat is, to the eye of a botanist, not a fruit, but a synconium, a specialized stem enclosing female flowers, sometimes fertilized, sometimes not. Only the male caprifig has both male and female flowers, and it's inedible.

Calimyrna figs, the most commercially important variety, must be fertilized by fig wasps carrying male pollen from the caprifig, or they drop off the tree before they ripen. Other figs blossom, swell, and ripen inside their specialized stem, not so much André Gide's "closed rooms where marriages are made" as unvisited harems where brides in their thousands sweeten without ever noticing that something's missing.

Figs are erotic. In the ancient world, and figs are among the most ancient of fruits, they were a symbol of peace and prosperity: "Judah and Israel dwelt safely, every man under his vine and his fig tree." But figs were also a symbol of female fertility. And both the phallic god Priapus, and Dionysus, the god of intoxication, count figs, as well as grapes, among their attributes.

I can't help but suspect that the real reason we don't eat more fresh figs is our culture's long-standing repression of pleasure at the table, its deeply held idea that it's bad to really enjoy eating, its certainty that food must be sanitized, processed, and controlled before it's safe to eat.

Surprise. Guess where fresh figs sit in the new pictures of nutritional virtue? They're in the second-largest, eat-a-lot of this band of the food rainbow. They taste good. They're good for you: no fat, a gram of protein, eight grams of carbohydrate, 2.5 grams of fibre, 40 milligrams of calcium, 2.5 milligrams of vitamin C.

You'll find them in markets spottily throughout the fall. Don't buy them if they're rock hard, dry, have flattened sides, splits, or signs of mould, or if they smell sour. Ripe figs give readily to gentle pressure, but aren't mushy. Eat them as soon as you can after bringing them home.

My friend Mary's father raised the most amazing figs—green, with pink inside, that ripened on his trees by the bucketful. After eating them fresh and grilling them, we put some of them up against the winter— although none of my jars made it past October.

Fig Preserves with Lime and Mint

1 lb. (500 g) fresh figs
1 cup (250 mL) sugar
1 Tbsp. (15 mL) grated lime rind
$\frac{1}{3}$ cup (75 mL) lime juice
3 Tbsp. (45 mL) finely chopped fresh mint

In a heavy-bottomed saucepan, combine the figs, sugar, lime rind, and lime juice. Bring to a boil over medium heat. Reduce heat to a simmer and cook until thickened, about 20 minutes. Stir in the mint and then ladle the mixture into sterilized jars. Process in a boiling water bath for 10 minutes.

Makes two 8-oz. (250-mL) jars.

Fine as Toast

LISSA SAID IT AND THE REST OF US LAUGHED, ALL FOUR AT ONCE, at the absurdity. She said: "I just need a nice cup of tea and I'll be fine as toast."

Everybody knows you can't be fine as toast. You can be warm as toast. You can be toast, which means finished, cooked, your schemes turned into so much fodder for someone else's mouth. You might possibly be fine as toast and tea, premiere comfort food of the Anglo world. But can you be fine as toast? No. Or at least those of us tucked up in the great communal sleeping bag of clichés can't. Fine as toast is jarring. It lands with the thud you might expect from something that's been dropped like a hot beet. It's like a fine kettle of turnips, or a bucket of beer in the sleeper's face.

This is more than just habit of language. Lately there has been a bit of charring around the edges of toast, something that isn't fine at all. You will find one statement of the toast problem in semiotician Arthur Asa Berger's essay "About the House: Cultural Studies." Berger believes that toast is a cover-up for the pathetic quality of our bread. "The existence of the toaster implies the existence of sliced bread," he writes, and not just of sliced bread, but of mechanized and standardized bread. "The toaster represents a heroic attempt to redeem our packaged bread, to redeem the unredeemable. But the toaster is doomed to the continual repetition of

Adam and Eve's Fall, for an unregenerate bread cannot be saved. Every piece of toast is a tragedy."

Although they were often made from the spongiest of processed white breads, I remember nothing tragic at all about the toast fingers my mother made for dipping into soft-boiled eggs. The two strips in the middle with crusts only on the short ends were best. But they were all crisp on the surface, yielding on the inside, soft with butter, coated in running egg yolk, salty and buttery. When I think of those toast fingers I always imagine sunshine, although the odds are that on the West Coast of B.C. there were more rainy days with toast fingers than sunny ones. But sunshine is in the nature of toast. Along with butter, honey, jam, and peanut butter, we spread contentment on toast.

It may be that the thing that's not so fine about toast is not mass-produced bread. Perhaps we should look instead to the squat little machines with the slots where sliced bread fits so neatly. Toasters, you see, are instruments of the devil.

I write this from the perspective of someone whose toaster died last summer. I have forgotten the exact date, but September 1 marks the day that we put it in the basement, bearing dire warnings on Post-it notes, so our cat-sitter would not be lured to an early grave while we were away on holiday. It's still there. This is not because I'm especially fond of the fallback position our household has taken on toast—the broiler in the oven. It's because I haven't had the time and the car and the will all at the same time. The only time I care about the broken toaster is when the toast burns. This happens when I put the toast in and go away to do other things, as decades of tuition at the hands of pop-up toasters have taught me to do. At its worst, I open the door on blackened crusts, realizing in quick succession that a) the eggs are cooked, b) the bacon is cooked, and c) those were the last four pieces of bread.

When I can remind myself not to do anything else at the same time, I like not having a toaster. Waiting for bread to turn brown is a pleasant task, just long enough to take a break from doing anything at all, not long enough to get boring. You can slow right down, making toast. After all, before the twentieth century got its hands on toast, the essence of toast was leisure.

To study the meaning of toast we must turn to the British, who yield to no nation in their toast enthusiasm, even if they do insist on serving it stone cold in a little rack. How British is toast? Food writer Elizabeth David, who devotes a full chapter of her book *English Bread and Yeast Cookery* to toast, reports that when the Duke of Wellington returned to England after six years away subduing Napoleon, his first order at Ship's Inn was for "an unlimited supply of buttered toast."

David believes that the English are particularly attuned to toast not because of the staleness of bread in remote villages—a theory proposed by one author—but because of "the open fires and coal ranges," in England. "For toasting bread in front of the fire and the bars of the coal-burning range there were dozens of different devices," David writes. "Museums of domestic life are crammed with them, Victorian cookery books show any number of designs." Can't you just see Victorian families sitting around making toast by the fireside in the late afternoon? How pleasant, how relaxed. How unlike our lives.

Despite the pop-up toaster, we moderns suffer the daily torments of the demon of business. We will know its full triumph on the day we decide that the best way to cook—hell, the only way, given how busy we are—is to put prepackaged frozen meals in a microwave oven. We might be better able to see what is going on here if we still spelled "busy" with an "i," the way they did in Middle English. Somehow the narrow, squeezed vowel, and the heightened similarity of "bisy" and "dizzy," exposes the state of bisiness for what it is: constant preoccupation with doing the next thing. The devilry of a toaster, and specifically a pop-up toaster, is the encouragement it offers to do two things at once. This is all very well if the objective is getting to work, fed, in the shortest possible time. But what function does it serve on Saturday morning, other than keeping us bisy?

The first electric toaster, marketed by the Crompton Company of Chelmsford, England, in 1893, changed only the source of heat. It demanded every bit as much attention to toast making as a coal fire. The McGraw Electric Company of Minneapolis, Minnesota, introduced the first pop-up in 1926. You set the timer, and the toast popped up when the time ran out. Proctor introduced the first smart toaster in 1930—its sensors responded to the surface temperature of the bread. That was the end of concentrating on the toast, despite the continued survival of old wing-style toasters in student apartments. Once you had achieved a pop-up toaster, you could put the toast in and completely forget about it, running no greater risk than coming back to find it cold.

Elizabeth David doesn't have an electric toaster, and demonstrates a proper wariness of toasters as "machines with which I cannot be doing."

I understand the sentiment. But I will not be scouring the antique stores for a set of toasting forks, although I can't swear I wouldn't buy some if they came my way. What I'm really looking for is ways to be less bisy; my life still consists of too much doing and not enough toasting. So I plan to continue crouching by the oven door, watching bread turn brown, feeling the tile floor under my bare feet. Being, shall we say, fine as toast.

Hot Pepper Masochism

WHAT A FINE, ELEGANT MASOCHISM WE PRACTISE, EATING CHILI peppers. Safe, comfortable, at ease in some spice-fragrant restaurant, with all of the means at hand to satisfy our hunger, we deliberately eat food that contains enough hot peppers to burn, and then sit there, intimately aware, in a roomful of strangers, of the shocking, delightful sensations in our mouths.

Is masochism too strong a word? The pain is certainly real. Chemical analysis tells us that tissue really is being injured. Hot peppers (capsicums) come in roughly two thousand varieties, and trade in them now surpasses trade in *Piper nigrum*, the black pepper Christopher Columbus was looking for when he sailed west. What makes them hot is capsaicin (pronounced cap-SAY-i-cin), a colourless, odourless chemical fire that can burn the skin in strong concentrations, and is especially painful if it reaches the eyes.

The concentration of capsaicin in any particular pepper is expressed in Scoville units, a measure named after pharmacologist Wilbur Scoville. In 1912, he devised a set of tests in which he gave subjects a drink of ground, dried chili peppers, alcohol, water, and sugar. If it burned their mouths, he diluted the drink with more water until he finally came up with a mixture that didn't burn at all.

Scoville units express the ratio of chili to water. The higher the number, the more water it takes to neutralize the pepper. Because the heat of individual chilies varies according to the growing conditions of the plant and how ripe the chili is—heat increases as the chili ripens—heats are normally expressed as a range of Scoville units. An ancho chili has 1,000 Scoville units of burn, a jalapeno has 2,500 to 5,000, a cayenne has 30,000 to 50,000 Scoville units, and habaneros—the hottest commercially grown pepper in the world—tops the scale at 100,000 to 300,000.

So why does one of us sit transported by the heat of a habanero while another is screaming for mercy after a mere jalapeno? Part of it is developing a tolerance for the heat. The rest is the ability to turn hot pepper pain into hot pepper pleasure. You will find what is still the definitive discussion of why people eat hot food in *Peppers: The Cultivated Capsicums,* an encyclopedic work written and illustrated by Texan and hot pepper authority Jean Andrews. Quoting the work of psychologists Paul Rozin and Deborah Schiller, Andrews tells us that the person who loves chili feels exactly the same thing as the person who hates chili: burning. But people who like hot peppers like the burn. It's what they do with it that's interesting. It appears that people who eat hot peppers are exploiting the same scare mechanism as people who go to horror movies or climb mountains or jump out of planes—activities that Rozin and Schiller lump together with hot pepper eating as "benignly masochistic" and "uniquely human."

What you do when you eat hot peppers is startle your body, convince it that something is seriously wrong, then make it stay put while you take pleasure in the very thing that has your eyes watering, your forehead beading with sweat, and your nose running. The pleasure lies in the fact that all of the defensive responses can be ignored with impunity. Digestive discomfort may lie ahead, but eating hot peppers is really not dangerous or life-threatening. It leads, in fact, to the sublime activity called "mouth surfing." That's the phrase author Andrew Weil, (*Marriage of the Sun and Moon: A Quest for Unity in Consciousness; The Natural Mind*), uses for the activity of the experienced pepper eater, who eats just enough hot peppers to keep crossing the line of pain into pleasure. People who like hot peppers, Weil writes, break into a state of "high consciousness," the sort of state we all might inhabit if all the nattering details of life could be permanently cut away with a capsicum sword. For as long as a meal lasts, they "glide along on the strong stimulation, experiencing it as something between pleasure and pain."

If we are willing to stretch the edges of the word "masochistic," to apply it not only to sexual but also to gustatory pleasures, reached through pain, then mouth surfing with hot peppers is surely masochism. It is also one of the male forms. That person at the table who takes pride in eating food so hot it makes him cry is almost always a man. Be honest here: when you call up the image of a contestant at a chili cook-off, whom do you see? Publisher Robert Speigel puts out forty thousand copies of *Whole Chile Pepper* magazine in Albuquerque, New Mexico. Forty per cent of its subscribers are male, which is disproportionately large for a magazine with recipes in it. Even in these days of changing roles, cooking breaks down on gender lines, Speigel says. "Usually the husband has some area that's his and often it's grilling and making chili." It may seem incongruous, then, that Jean Andrews is chief among the hot pepper experts. But Andrews' work reveals a thoroughly macho pepper enthusiast, someone who thinks public contests to see who can eat the most hot peppers are "fun, sorta like a night out to watch someone being burned at the stake."

Hot pepper eaters do build tolerance, and learn to eat capsaicin in quantities that would blister the mouths of the uninitiated. In 1973, in London, a friend awed me by eating a whole, hot, sour pickled lime in one mouthful. A tiny piece of it, buried deep in rice and chapati, was enough to jolt my tender mouth. Eventually it's a question of how far you have to go to get the thrill.

A colleague who admits to some knowledge of mouth surfing went bungie jumping on a recent trip to New Zealand. With his ankles tied together and attached to a giant bungie cord, he leapt off a 150-foot-high bridge into a gorge—a two-second, headfirst fall toward a shallow river in a stony rock bed. While he was poised at the end of the gangplank, waiting for the countdown, he realized that every fibre of his body had begun to speak to him with startling clarity. It was saying: "Don't do this." Only his mind, for reasons that looked increasingly fatuous, wanted to make the jump. Ego pushed.

He'd been told beforehand that the first six feet were the hard part. He claims that this apparently witless statement is true. Once you've committed yourself, the only thing left to do is enjoy the adrenalin surge.

At the edge of the pepper abyss, the body also announces its resistance. Without benefit of bungie cord, the hot pepper eater fills with a sudden physical awareness, a powerful warning, and overrules it, listening instead to the siren song: "Make the jump, take the leap, the pain you accept transforms, on the other side of this you'll find ecstasy."

When the pepper rush is over, these turn out to be only slippery words, radiant with possibility, hard to get a grip on. But for as long as the mouth surfing lasts, that song is as clear and sparkling as a fish made of ice, melting in a river of flame.

It takes about a dozen mussels to satisfy one person, less if you serve them over pasta. This is a very seductive sauce. If you're not serving it over pasta, have a good loaf of bread on hand to sop it up. Any self-respecting hot pepper masochist has a favorite bottled hot sauce. Mine is Marie Sharp's Grapefruit Pulp Habanero Pepper Sauce from Belize.

Coconut Milk Mussels as Hot as You Want Them

4 dozen mussels
3 Tbsp. (45 mL) vegetable oil
1 cup (250 mL) finely chopped mild onion
1-inch (2.5-cm) piece of ginger, peeled and chopped fine
1 Tbsp. (15 mL) finely chopped jalapeno pepper
1 5.6-oz. (165-mL) can coconut milk
hot sauce to taste
¼ cup (50 mL) finely chopped fresh basil
4 tsp. (20 mL) finely chopped fresh mint

Check the mussels and discard any with shells that gape open and won't close when tapped.

Heat the oil in a large, shallow frying pan that has a lid over medium heat. Add the onion, ginger, and jalapeno, and cook, stirring frequently, for 5 minutes, or until the onion has softened.

Add the coconut milk and heat until it simmers. Add hot sauce to taste. Add the mussels, stirring well to coat. Add the basil and mint. Put the lid on and cook for 3 to 5 minutes. Mussels are cooked when the shells pop open.

Serves four as a main course, eight as an appetizer.

Why Chocolate Is Evil

"I SHOULDN'T," WE SAY, AND THEN WE DO. "DON'T TEMPT ME," we say, and then let a Belgian chocolate take us by the hand. We eat devil's food cake, and Death by Chocolate. "If chocolate is your downfall, you might as well enjoy the trip," reads the ad for chocolatier Ferrero Rocher.

Chocolate is not evil, of course, no more than turnips are evil. Unwelcome at times, yes. But for as long as Europeans have known about chocolate, the dark substance has radiated an evil glow. Chocolate is a temptress. Chocolate seduces dieters away from their salads. Chocolate is something we eat purely for pleasure. A plant product with a reasonable amount of protein (a little less than 10 per cent in baking chocolate) and small amounts of potassium, iron, and phosphorus to recommend it, chocolate forms an important part of no one's diet, and no deficiency diseases are caused by its absence. The sensation of pleasure, the dark, profound note of chocolate spreading over the tongue, is purely gratuitous.

Eating is a necessity, but gluttony is a sin. Wherever you draw the line, chocolate, the unnecessary, addictive food with a darkly sensual impact, is not likely to be on the right side.

Gluttony does not necessarily involve eating huge quantities of food (a point Margaret Horsfield established in a CBC radio documentary on the Seven Deadly Sins). It does mean caring too much about food—the way chocolate-dependent people can't stop being aware of a plate of brownies until all the brownies are gone. "It is not food, but the desire for food that is the cause of damnation," wrote the sixth century ascetic, Pope Gregory the Great. "The belly, when it is not restrained, destroys the virtues of the soul."

Every chocolate-dependent person knows how consuming the desire for chocolate can be. But there is more. Gluttony is located close to lust on the map of sin. Just above it, in fact. Gregory again: "It is plain to all that lust springs from gluttony, when in the very distribution of the members, the genitals appear placed beneath the belly. And hence when one is inordinately pampered, the other is doubtless excited to wantonness." The same sentiment was much more jovially put by Antonio Colmenero de Ledesma in his 1631 *Curioso tratado de la naturaleza y calidad del chocolate*, translated in 1640 by James Wadsworth (an ex-Jesuit who spent the bulk of his writing time on anti-Catholic treatises):

Twill make Old women Young and Fresh;
Create New Motions of the Flesh,
And cause them long for you know what,
If they but taste of chocolate.

That was certainly the hope of the Marquise de Pompadour, mistress to Louis XV, who, despite being one of history's most famous courtesans, was frigid—or as a biographer of her rival, Madame du Barry, wrote: "Pompadour's had been the paradox of some great concert pianist born with insufficient fingers." To add ardour to her cold nature, she drank truffle and celery soup washed down with chocolate every morning. Casanova drank chocolate in the mornings too, and thought it was as useful as champagne for amatory adventure. And Montezuma, the Aztec emperor who, much to his later regret, shared his chocolate with Cortés, drank fifty cups a day, and always had chocolate before going into his harem.

If your last mug of Nestlé's Quik didn't have any such results, perhaps it was lacking a few important ingredients. Montezuma's brew was a bitter draft that did not include sugar, but did include chili peppers, and quite probably some more intoxicating plant materials. In his 1985 book *The Cacahuatl Eater: Ruminations of an Unabashed Chocolate Addict*, Jonathan Ott suggests that Montezuma's main kick might have been psilocybin mushrooms. Ott (whose previous titles are *Hallucinogenic Plants of North America*, *Teonanacatl: Hallucinogenic Mushrooms of North America*, and *LSD: My Problem Child*, a translation of Albert Hofmann's *LSD: Mein Sorgenkind*) believes that not just the juice of magic mushrooms, but possibly morning glory seeds and an inebriating mint still drunk as a tea today were mixed into Aztec chocolate drinks.

Neither the Spanish, Portuguese, French, nor, as chocolate spread throughout seventeenth-century Europe, the English, were taking psilocybin mushrooms with their chocolate. Still, what they drank was far from the equivalent of a modern child's after-school cup of cocoa. The fashionable young "bloods" who hung out in London's somewhat unsavoury chocolate houses, gambling and fighting, drank their chocolate melted into wine and other spirits. Milk as a medium for dissolving the chocolate wasn't hit upon until around 1730.

Science has found two active chemicals in chocolate: theobromine and phenylethylamine. Theobromine is a cousin of caffeine, and just as likely to cause habituation, and cravings when the substance is withdrawn. Its name comes from the scientific name for the cacao plant, *Theobromia cacao*, meaning food of the gods. Like coffee, it is a stimulant, and makes the heart beat faster. Some people believe the stimulant effect accounts for chocolate's aphrodisiac reputation, a theory that doesn't explain the curious lack of such a reputation for coffee.

Theobromine in chocolate can have evil consequences, at least for horses. De Rigueur, a four-year-old gelding who won the Balmoral Handicap at Ascot in September 1987, was later disqualified when a routine urine test showed traces of the stimulant, left over from a Mars Bar the sweet-toothed thoroughbred had eaten the day before the race. No matter how innocent the source, the presence of theobromine still resulted in the loss of a $20,000 purse and a fine for the trainer.

Phenylethylamine, a relative of mescaline, is produced naturally in the body when people fall in love. Its presence in chocolate seems to offer the ultimate explanation for chocolate cravings, to say nothing of Valentine's Day chocolates. Unfortunately for such a tidy theory, research shows that phenylethylamine isn't present in chocolate in a large enough dose to have any effect on people.

No matter what its chemical basis, the connection of chocolate and evil continues. The first devil's food recipe appeared in 1905, about the time when chocolate and cocoa were first readily available to home cooks. In *The Dictionary of American Food and Drink*, John Mariani defines devil's food as "a cake, muffin, or cookie made with dark chocolate, so called because it is supposedly so rich and delicious that it must to a moralist, be somewhat sinful."

Common sense will tell us that if the devil really lives on chocolate, he would have had a hungry time before 1528, when Cortés brought it home to the court of Charles V. But I have my own reasons to suspect that chocolate suits the devil. As a chocolate-addicted child, I would eat anything chocolate, and not too much that wasn't. I drank chocolate milk and chocolate milkshakes. I ate chocolate ice cream, chocolate bars, fudge, and any form of boxed chocolates. I preferred dark chocolate, but if only milk chocolate was around, I ate that. As soon as I was old enough to cook, I mastered the family chocolate recipes, especially Aunt Esther's famous hot-water chocolate cake, with icing made from two squares of unsweetened chocolate.

But there were times when there was no chocolate in the house, and my weekly allowance, which was in any case only good for two chocolate bars, about a quarter of the amount my habit demanded, ran out. In the lowest of those moments, when the craving was strongest, I stole money from a little jar high on a kitchen shelf, a jar known as the church fund, because, when it was full of dimes, it was going to become a donation.

Dime after dime, pilfered, became a Neilson's Peppermint Roll, dark chocolate around a peppermint centre. The ritual of the fix was the same as for maraschino cherries: bite off the bottom, suck out the middle, then pop the chocolate shell and let it dissolve slowly over the tongue. I knew what company I was keeping when my hand dipped into the church fund, but I couldn't help it. I needed chocolate, with the same unarguable need of any addict. Between us, the devil and I must owe the United Church ten dollars.

I still make Aunt Esther's modest little scratch cake frequently, whenever there's a birthday, a celebration, or a summer dinner that needs something sweet and chocolate at the end. Now that I've memorized the recipe, and have a microwave oven to bring the butter to room temperature, I can get it in the oven in 15 minutes without turning a hair. For my money, when it's fresh out of the oven, cooled only enough that the icing doesn't melt and run, it's as good as any chocolate cake needs to be. The only change I've made is in the icing, which now contains six ounces of Belgian semi-sweet chocolate. Quality matters, both in the chocolate in the icing and the cocoa in the cake. My preference is for the smoother, darker, Dutch process cocoa, which has been treated with an alkali to remove some of its natural acidity.

Aunt Esther's Chocolate Cake

$^1/_2$ cup (125 mL) butter
1 cup (250 mL) sugar
2 eggs
$^1/_2$ cup (125 mL) cocoa
1 tsp. (5 mL) vanilla
$1^1/_2$ cups (375 mL) all-purpose flour
2 tsp. (10 mL) baking powder
1 tsp. (5 mL) baking soda
pinch of salt
$^1/_2$ cup (125 mL) milk
$^1/_2$ cup (125 mL) boiling water

Icing
6 oz. (175 g) Belgian semi-sweet chocolate
4 Tbsp. (60 mL) butter
1 cup (250 mL) icing sugar
1 tsp. (5 mL) vanilla
1–2 Tbsp. (15–25 mL) milk, if necessary

Preheat the oven to 350°F (180°C). Grease an 8-inch (20-cm) springform cake pan.

Cream the butter and sugar. Add the eggs one by one, beating until smooth. Add the cocoa and vanilla.

Sift the flour, baking powder, baking soda, and salt. Add to the butter mixture alternately with milk. Add the boiling water, mixing with a few quick strokes.

Bake for 40 to 50 minutes, or until a knife inserted in the centre comes out clean.

For the Icing: Melt the chocolate on low heat in the microwave and stir in the butter. Sift the icing sugar into the chocolate mixture. Add the vanilla. Add enough milk to bring the icing to spreading consistency.

Why Ginger Is Hot

THE BOY IN THE SUPERMARKET PRODUCE DEPARTMENT WAS maybe five years old, old enough to be asking so many questions that his parents had stopped hearing him. "What's this?" he asked, grabbing a knobby stem. When they didn't answer, he said, "I guess it's ginger," and put it down.

What a world we've traversed. When I was five, ginger was a dry powder in a dusty jar in the back of the spice shelf. It was used less often than cloves, more often than cayenne pepper. It went in gingerbread. Sometimes my mother made gingersnaps, but not often. I had no truck with powdered ginger. Musty and acrid in itself, it was also one of the flavours offered at dessert that could therefore have been chocolate, but wasn't. I would have traded a dozen gingerbread men for a single piece of fudge. Fresh ginger lay completely outside my world.

Ginger is hot, which is why I knew nothing about it. My family had very few culinary heat sources except black pepper, and none with the seductive pull of ginger. My mother was a cook in the good plain food tradition: chives and parsley, salt and pepper were the four corners of our world of herbs and spices. In this tradition food may satisfy you; it's not intended to excite you.

But ginger is hot. That's why the child in the produce department knew the answer to his own question. Every supermarket stocks fresh ginger now, and not just tired, wrinkled ginger either. Sometimes there's young Hawaiian ginger so vigorous, you think with a shock that if you planted it, it would grow again. Ginger is one of the great successes of crossover cuisine. Deep-fried crab ravioli would be naked without thin threads of ginger. Thai food, our most recent infatuation, does not exist without ginger, any more than East Indian or Chinese food. Heat is now popular, and ginger is hot.

A chemist can tell you that what makes ginger hot is two chemicals called zingerone and gingerol. The taste comes from other chemicals including cineol, borneol, geraniol, linalool, and farmasene.

But what makes ginger a hot commodity? It will not do to answer that people like hot things, that we're now more exposed to different cuisines, and so naturally ginger, one of the world's triad of top hot things—black pepper, chili pepper, ginger—is hot. People do not, in fact, like hot things, not until their culture tells them to. Psychologist Paul Rozin, in a paper titled "The Use of Characteristic Flavourings in Human Culinary Practice," writes that hunting and gathering peoples rarely spice their food with any of the big three, even when they're available. Give a child, an adult new to the taste, or an animal a hot spice, and the first response is aversion.

People do become habituated to hot tastes and then come to crave them. Animals don't, even animals as close to us in taste mechanisms and innate preferences as rats. You can't get a rat to like hot tastes even if you feed it chili from the moment of conception. We know this because Rozin fed pregnant rats chili-laced lab chow, then fed their offspring with the same until they were seven months old. When he tested them, "all the rats preferred chili-free chow and after a few days of choice ate virtually no chili diet."

But in most of the world's cuisines, one or more of the hot spices dominates and, in combination with a few other flavours, defines the food and gives it a characteristic taste. Mexicans have chili and tomatoes; the Chinese have ginger and chilies; East Indians have ginger, chilies, black pepper, and a few more hot spices to boot.

Here is another puzzle: The broad Anglo-Saxon stream that fed into my mother's cooking was once fragrant with ginger. Ginger came to England with the Romans, who loved it as much as pepper, and for the same blunt reason: the burn. Pliny the Elder felt moved to inform them that ginger was not, contrary to popular opinion, the root of the pepper plant. (Why do I get the feeling that if the Roman legions were here today they'd be down at McDonald's smothering their chips in ketchup and salt?) The ginger they were eating was not fresh ginger, by the way. It was grown in India and China, peeled, sun-dried, shipped along the spice route, getting more valuable as it travelled.

By the fifteenth century, what British food writer Elizabeth David calls "ginger mania" was in full sway. You could trade a pound of ginger for a sheep, and ground ginger sat with the salt and pepper in its own shaker at the table. "In every other recipe of the time one finds instructions to mix together 'canelle (cinnamon), pepir, gyngere and safroun,'" she writes in *Salts, Spices and Aromatics in the English Kitchen*. Then the taste for ginger, and for spicy food in general, began to fade. By the eighteenth century, the great tide of ginger that once flavoured every course had ebbed away until its major use was in desserts and drinks.

That's exactly where I first found it, 250 years later: in gingerbread, ginger ale, and in the language. The acrid beige powder in the spice jar was far from vigorous, vital, or lively, but I knew that to "put some ginger into it" meant to heat something up, to give it energy. Ginger is spirited, like redheads, who are often called Ginger despite the fact that dirty blond is a closer colour match. To "ginger up" means to enliven; it may come from the practice of "figging" a horse—using ginger as a suppository to make the horse hold its tail high—or from putting ginger in drinks. A ginger, at least according to the *Slang Thesaurus*, is "a thieving prostitute."

One of the less obvious words left behind by the ginger craze is "racy," from the Portuguese word *raices* (root), which is what they called ginger. The word came into English because the Portuguese, once they reached India, were able to take the ginger trade away from the spice-road traders and Venetian merchants who had monopolized it for 1,500 years.

Why did Europeans turn away from hot spices? In his book *Ginger East to West*, Bruce Cost speculates that once ginger was no longer expensive, and therefore useless as a status symbol, people no longer wanted it. What mattered more was being able to afford food fresh enough that it didn't need heavy spicing. And then there's the matter of ginger being hot. "In England, as the lusty Elizabethans gave way to the Puritans, and later the Victorians, the unabashed use of aphrodisiacs became frowned upon," writes Cost. "Many aspects of life that were once 'spicy' or 'racy' were simply no longer accepted."

It's amazing, when you think of it, what exquisitely sensitive creatures the Victorians must have been, to grasp so surely the connection between gustatory pleasure and sexual pleasure, the dangerous proximity of receptors in the brain's pleasure centres, the dread possibility of spillover.

What makes ginger hot now? I wouldn't rule out the possibility that we are looking for an aphrodisiac. Much depends on your definition. Experts as early as Dioscordes, writing in the first century, agreed that ginger was "of an heating and digesting quality." Joseph Kadans in his *Modern Encyclopedia of Herbs* writes that ginger "is a stimulant, tending to excite the glands to action." The sixteenth-century herbalist John Gerard wrote that it "provoketh Venerie"—the pursuit of sexual pleasure. We habitually think of passion as burning, so if heat is what you mean, then ginger is hot. As with most energy, the choice of how you direct it is yours.

The best way to grate ginger is to use a rasp. Position it over a bowl to catch the juice. This is a great summer supper if you have the presence of mind to poach the fish in the morning. The kitchen stays cool, and dinner goes together in a flash.

Gingered Fish Tacos with Guacamole

1 lb. (500 g) cod or other white fish
2 cups (500 mL) chicken or vegetable stock
2 tsp. (10 mL) grated fresh ginger
2 tsp. (10 mL) lime juice
8 soft wheat tortillas

Guacamole
1 avocado, peeled and chopped
1 tomato, chopped
1 Tbsp. (15 mL) lime juice
$^{1}/_{2}$ tsp. (2 mL) salt
2 Tbsp. (30 mL) chopped fresh cilantro
hot sauce to taste

2 cups (500 mL) arugula

In a frying pan with a lid, bring the chicken stock to a simmer. Add the fish and poach, covered, for 5 to 7 minutes, or until the flesh is firm and opaque. Remove the fish from the poaching liquid and cool.

Flake the fish. In a small bowl, combine the ginger and lime juice, then add the flaked fish and mix gently.

If you have a gas stove, heat each flour tortilla directly over the burner until it puffs, turning once or twice. On an electric stove, use a heavy frying pan over medium-high heat, turning once or twice and pressing the edges of the tortillas with a clean dish towel to make them puff.

For the Guacamole: Mix the avocado, tomato, lime juice, salt, cilantro, and hot sauce.

To assemble: place one-eighth of the fish mixture into each tortilla. Top with one-eighth of the guacamole, and of the arugula.

Makes four servings.

Mangoes and Apples

IF YOU WANT TO GRASP THE DIFFERENCE BETWEEN LIFE IN THE tropics and life in the temperate zones, look no further than our fruit. We have apples. They have mangoes. There's no use bemoaning the fact that it isn't fair. You can't get a mango tree to survive in a climate that is subject to frosts, and that's all there is to it.

In India, 70 per cent of orchards are devoted to mangoes. Mangoes are eaten both green and ripe, raw and cooked, pickled, candied, and made into juice. Many families have a backyard mango tree, as we have backyard apple trees. Children learn the ways of thievery with mangoes, the way we learn to steal apples.

Like apples, mangoes have hundreds of varieties. Like the apple market, the mango market is dominated by a handful of giants: Alphonso and Mulgoa in India, Julie and Peter in the West Indies, and Hayden in Florida are the Macs and Granny Smiths of warmer climes.

The single biggest difference between mangoes and apples as edible commodities is perishability. For all but the luxury market, the mango season is over shortly after the trees stop bearing. We store apples in refrigerated warehouses and are still eating last year's crop when this year's crop is being picked.

In all other respects, you are at liberty to think of mangoes as the apples of the East. This is, undeniably, a leap, especially if you happen to be holding a gold-and-red mango in your hand, pressing into the smooth, leathery skin to test for softness, smelling the scent of flowers at the stem end. What a voluptuous thing to find in your lunch bag every day.

A professor of Sanskrit told me that when he was a boy in Bombay he stole mangoes, that it was tolerated, and that there was even a certain amount of grudging respect for cunning small thieves. He didn't get sick on green mangoes, as boys here do on green apples, because Indian boys eat green mangoes dipped in fiery mixture of salt, chili pepper, and black pepper. "You can't eat more than two," the professor said.

Bombay is famous for its mangoes. People there feel more excitement when the mangoes ripen than we do when the apples ripen, at least partly because mangoes still have a season and apples don't. Absence makes the palate grow fonder too. Many Indians think it's unhealthy to eat mangoes out of season, which is fortunate, because out-of-season mangoes are available only in big cities, at high prices. "If someone were to say that they wanted to taste a mango again before they died, then that would be taken very seriously," the professor told me, hastening to add that mangoes are not really a common deathbed request, just an example. And an interesting concept. Has anyone ever asked for just one more taste of a Granny Smith before death?

The sensuality of mangoes is of course the difference. Mango pie and mango crisp sound odd, but not impossible. But how appealing is apple ice cream? Or cold apple soup?

I first ate cold mango soup on the River Terrace at the Oriental Hotel in Bangkok. We had just come back from seven hungry days in Burma, from eating in restaurants where most of the food and all of the beer was already "finiss" when we walked in the door. Thai plenty had not yet lost its power to amaze. The soup was served in a wide, flat bowl, an expanse of orange broken by a sprig of mint. It had vodka in it. It was sweet and smooth and as cold as a bullet. I've made cold mango soup a few times since then, and have come to like it even more. If you add a cup of heavy cream, it will be voluptuous. If you use yogurt instead it will be lighter and tarter. Lemon is good, and mint. We don't often have vodka, so I've never found myself with a bottle of vodka and enough mangoes to make soup at the same time, but I have made soup from gin and mangoes, and it was, as the Norwegians say, plenty good enough.

Getting the pulp of seven mangoes—enough for four or five bowls of soup—into the work bowl of a food processor is, of course, messier than peeling apples. My preferred method demands surrender of the idea of dry hands: peel the mango, carefully cut away the flesh until nothing is left but the pit and the fibrous hairs attached to it, then grasp the pit and give it a good squeeze, letting the juice run out between the fingers of your closed fist.

Only in blossom time can apples match the sensuality of mangoes. Mango blossoms and apple blossoms are both welcome signs of spring: delicate, fleeting, and entirely appropriate as the symbol of young love. "Cherry pink and apple blossom white," sings Pérez Prado, the Mambo King, linking spring, love, and blossoms. Both Tab Hunter and Wayne Newton have promised to "be with you in apple blossom time."

The one time in Indian ritual when you absolutely must have mango blossoms, says the professor of Sanskrit, is the spring festival in honour of Kama. "He's a minor god, a kind of Cupid," the professor says. Kama's quiver holds five arrows, all of them blossoming branches that he shoots at people to make them fall in love. Don't picture a chubby cherub. Think of the tall, handsome son of Vishnu the preserver, second member in the Hindu trinity, and his consort, Lakshmi, goddess of beauty, wealth, and pleasure. Think of the god of love, the god who lends his name to the Kama Sutra.

If mango blossoms are linked to Kama in popular Indian thought, apples here are firmly linked to Eve. In fact, we don't really know what fruit Eve ate in the Garden of Eden. In Genesis, where she's quoted, the errant woman is maddeningly vague, describing the forbidden fruit only as "the fruit of the tree which is in the midst of the garden." Muslim theologians have suggested that the fruit in question was a fig. We grew up imagining it as an apple. Scholars tell us it is most unlikely that the serpent tempted Eve with a Golden Delicious, but oh the difference it makes to believe that it might have been so.

Apples have a crisp, businesslike, go-to-work taste, a dutiful wholesomeness expressed in the old advice for staying out of the presence of doctors. Eve's gesture with the apple is one we ourselves have performed casually and often: You want a bite of my apple?

Imagine if the apple had been a mango. Suddenly the temperature in the garden shoots up ten degrees, and the leaves of the mango tree take on an intense green. Eve offers Adam a bite of orange flesh, juice glistening from the ridges left where the skin was pulled back. From the shade of the mango tree, the snake presides over the site of his first big triumph. It would have been a whole different deal.

Why Mushrooms Are Scary

ARE YOU WILLING TO PLACE A HAND OVER A DINNER PLATE AND swear that you have never had a moment's hesitation in the presence of a mushroom? Then, I would say flatly, you are lying. Mushrooms are scary. If, as Swift would have it, "he was a bold man that first eat an oyster," then what do we call the first human being to bite into a mushroom?

Under no more than casual observation, oysters show themselves to be related to clams and mussels, evidently alive, and clearly safe food for seabirds. Mushrooms, on the other hand, are so distinct from more usual forms of life that they have a category all their own—we divide living things into animals, plants, bacteria, amoebae, and fungi. Furthermore, they have a disconcerting habit of growth. They spring full-blown out of the ground, or out of a rotting tree stump. There is a reason for all those clichés about mushrooming growth. From a barely visible clump of hairs, an oyster mushroom can grow to a cluster a foot across in twenty-four hours, so fast you can almost watch it grow.

This must have been disconcerting to our oldest ancestors, who faced tougher real-life food tests than finding the right kind of eggplant at the market. One day, you cross a clearing in the woods and it is grass; the next day mushrooms have sprung up all over the field, or, more eerie still, sprung up in circles and formed "fairy rings" on the meadow. That mushrooms get eaten at all is a testimony to humanity's single-minded dedication to the task of finding out how much of the environment is, strictly speaking, edible.

There must have been some sobering moments along the way to culinary enjoyment of mushrooms. Of the 32 poisonous species (out of an estimated 40,000 we recognize as mushrooms) some are so toxic they put arsenic and strychnine to shame. Which means, of course, that mushrooms can be used as a weapon. *Amonita phalloides*, the deadly amanita, or death cup, accounts for 90 per cent of deaths from mushroom poisoning. In one of the best-known nonaccidental poisonings, Agrippina mixed a few into her husband's, the Emperor Claudius's, dinner to clear the way to the throne for her son Nero.

No wonder the guileless button mushroom is the only one widely eaten in North America. The button mushroom, *Agaricus bisporus*, was first cultivated in France at the beginning of the eighteenth century, hence its name *champignon de Paris*. The British, who are generally indifferent to mushrooms, liked it, and eventually exported it to the U.S. Then, in 1926, Lewis Downing of Downington, Pennsylvania, discovered pure white spores growing among his brown mushrooms. The North American love of white food did the rest. Pennsylvania is still the centre for button mushrooms, and buttons are still the centre of the North American mushroom world. Mushroom growers in B.C. sell 30 million pounds of agaricus mushrooms a year. In 1990, oyster mushroom sales were only 425,000 pounds; shiitake mushrooms, 75,000 pounds.

Blame our British heritage for the market dominance of button mushrooms. Already a mushroom-phobic people, the Brits never developed an equivalent of the peasant cuisines of Europe, or in other words, hunger apparently never drove them into the arms of cepes and chanterelles.

Instead, they cleaved closely to the line laid down by the *Grete Herball*, of 1526. After setting out that "there be two manners of them; one manner is deedly and sleeth them that eateth of them and be called tode stooles, and the other dooth not," the *Herball* calls even the non-poisonous mushrooms "peryllous and dredful to eate," and offers this general recommendation: "it is good to eschew them." When the already mushroom-wary pilgrims came to Plymouth Rock, they found forests full of mushrooms that the Native peoples didn't eat. The same was true on the West Coast, where abundant food supplies are invoked as the reason neither Coastal nor Interior Native peoples seem to have eaten the cepes, morels, chanterelles, and matsutakes growing there. (Some Interior bands now harvest mushrooms, but only the European varieties. If a pre-contact taste test had established which were edible, surely they would also eat the locally occurring pine mushrooms, the matsutakes that the Japanese love well enough to try to track by satellite.)

Other countries still happily import tons of North American chanterelles and matsutakes every year—mushrooms we almost never see in our Canadian markets.

But there's another reason that the button mushroom lords it over the produce shelves: it is easily cultivated. And in the world of mushrooms, that is no small advantage. Despite years of research, no one has figured out how to grow "mycorrhizal" mushrooms without the trees they live in mutual benefit with: boletus with conifers, oak and beech, and matsutake with the pine tree.

Here we must take a detour into the life story of mushrooms.

Unless you're a mushroom expert, or a botanist, it's more complicated than you think. For example, that oyster mushroom sautéing in olive oil is far from a complete mushroom plant. In fact, it bears the same relationship to the mushroom plant as an apple does to an apple tree. What we think of as mushrooms are just the product of a bunch of hairs in a party mood.

The living, regenerating mushroom is an underground network of hairlike strands. They spread through the soil, or push between cells of rotting tree trunks, feeding and waiting until conditions seem right for launching spores. Then the mushroom sends out what botanists call a "fruiting body," on which spores can mature, and eventually be released.

When commercial growers want to seed a mushroom bed, they find a mushroom they like, then let its threads spread throughout a specially enriched growing medium. Once the mushroom's threads have spread out and filled the bed, they cut thousands of identical slices of these threads and send them out to growers. Put into a bed, the threads regenerate, while the grower simulates a dry night somewhere warm. For nine to ten days, no light touches the mushroom beds, and the temperature is 27°C (80°F). Then the grower brings on spring: lights come on for 12 hours a day, temperature drops to 18°C (64°F), and the humidity soars to 85 to 90 per cent. Two days later, the black plastic that covers the bed, pierced with holes every five inches, begins to "blush," as the mushroom growers say. You can see a few buds the night before. The next morning, the bed's covered in mushrooms.

Mushroom beds will continue to produce as long as there are nutrients left in the growth medium, but there are only two commercially viable blushes before the pounds of mushrooms produced drop precipitously in quality and uniformity.

In the wild, some mushrooms live for a hundred years, sending up fruiting bodies in their season. Some of them, like the native North American oyster mushroom, a cousin of the strains now being raised commercially, are parasites that kill the trees they grow on. Others grow only in dead wood. Combine overnight growth with rotted wood and you have a troubling image. Add an underground network that feeds in the dark and it's enough to make fruiting bodies like us nervous.

Perhaps that's why mushrooms show up in literature mostly as a symbol of the brevity of human life. Even a button mushroom can serve as a memento mori, reminding us that as long as it may seem between paydays, in the larger scheme of things, death for each of us is just around the corner.

"Man is born in vanity and sin; he comes into the world like morning mushrooms, soon thrusting up their heads into the air . . . and as soon they turn into dust and forgetfulness," wrote Jeremy Taylor, chaplain to Charles I, in *The Rule and Exercises of Holy*

Dying, in 1651. Taylor's sensibilities were no doubt sharpened by the recent execution of the King. But John Donne was only echoing common sentiment, in his sermon on Eternity, when he wrote: "Methusalem, with all his hundreds of years, was but a mushroom of a night's growth, to this day."

Medlars

IT'S BEEN YEARS SINCE I'VE FELT THE PECULIAR ANXIETY OF introducing a new love to my social circle. But now that I've fallen for medlars, it's all come rushing back. I'm protective and apprehensive, and I know in advance that not everyone will be charmed.

I first caught wind of medlars several years ago, while looking up melons in the pages of Waverley Root's food encyclopedia. My eyes strayed, inadvertently, to the entry on medlars, and I was entranced. So on the grey day in early November when I saw a medlar tree in Vancouver's VanDusen Botanical Garden, I felt at once a surge of excitement, mixed with a touch of caution.

Chaucer ate medlars, and mentions them in *The Canterbury Tales*. Shakespeare makes a dirty medlar joke in *Romeo and Juliet* (Act II, Scene 1). Until some years into the nineteenth century, any self-respecting British grocer carried them as one of the treats of the Christmas season. Then medlars fell so completely out of favour that most of us have never heard of them. A 150-year gap in a resumé is bound to raise eyebrows; even more so when the resumé belongs to a British festive food. We furnish our holiday tables with items as odd as plum pudding and mincemeat. Surely if we had liked medlars in the first place we would have kept in touch.

Rumour said that medlars had never been troublesome, just

dull, especially once bananas and oranges came to the table. Medlars had traditionally been made into jellies and desserts, or most commonly, eaten after dinner, with port. After the 1880s, when inexpensive sugar filled whatever need there once had been for medlars' sweetness, they dropped off the bottom of the shopping list.

The VanDusen medlar tree was getting on in years and rested its weight on a wooden support. The leaves had begun to drop, revealing the fruit—glowing bronze balls about the size of a hefty new potato, stippled with slightly darker freckles. They were as hard as green apples, but open at the blossom end, like an apple that for some reason hadn't pulled a blanket of flesh over its core.

They were autumnal, enchanting, a fruit from my own culinary tradition with all the allure of a stranger. I picked one. Then I took my medlar home and waited for it to blet.

Of all the astonishing things Waverley Root wrote about medlars, bletting had to be the best. It would be enough that blet is an irresistibly comic word, begging for someone to put on a British accent and bray, "Do come over, our medlars have bletted." But there's much more. British botanist John Lindley borrowed the word from French and used it, in 1835, in his book *An Introduction to the Natural System of Botany*. "After the period of ripeness," he wrote, "most fleshy fruits undergo a new form of alteration. Their flesh either rots or blets." Most fruit rots. Persimmons, pears, and some apples, those that must be stored before they turn sweet and smooth-textured, blet.

Good news for boomers, you say? Those who find themselves undeniably ripe, but not yet ready to decay, have been taking comfort in the idea of bletting for centuries, ever since Chaucer, pointing to medlars, wrote: "Til we be roten, can we not be rype?"

Before Chaucer's time most people didn't use the word medlar. They called it "open-arse," or "open-erse," or sometimes "open-ers." One theory on the medlar's disappearance is that the tender sensibilities of the nineteenth century found its anatomy too rude for family dinners.

"What might have brought a blush to mediaeval maidens was never allowed to trouble the sensibilities of their Victorian descendants," James Driver writes in the English magazine *Country Life*. "For while the infamous Dr. Bowdler was furiously removing every line of Shakespeare's that he felt might give offense to the gentlewomen of the house, their gardeners were doing much the same to medlar trees."

My medlar looked innocuous enough. Even when a friend and I had talked our way into harvesting VanDusen's entire medlar crop for research, the sight of a few hundred medlars set in a cupboard to blet was more cute than arousing. Then one by one the medlars began to soften. The golden bronze skin faded to a dull brown, now darker than the freckles. The seeds, at first barely visible, became a clear pentagram.

It looked like blet to me. So I bought port and introduced the medlars to two of my old school friends and their spouses after our annual dinner. The reaction was polite but not enthusiastic. Next I dressed the medlars up with brie, dates, and bread, and introduced them to my family and to other friends. Some of the people who ate them, I suspect, would have voted with Thomas Gray, author of the famous *Elegy Written in a Country Church-yard:* "If there were nothing but medlars and blackberries in the world, I could very well consent to go without any at all."

Then, cleaning up a day or two after a medlar tasting, I was shocked to find that one of the medlars left on the serving plate had become tumescent, engorged. The wrinkles were gone. The skin was as smooth as a just-picked medlar, and now it shone again, in some places a dark wine red, in others, a rich purple brown with golden spots. The once recessed seeds had popped out. The pentagram was even more prominent. And the rim of the calyx had begun to leak a sweet, shiny juice.

I peeled it. The scent had sharpened. Instead of the muted applesauce smell, it was stronger and sweeter, the taste of apple-flavoured fermentation, but not the taste of a rotten apple. I felt, unmistakably, a little electric thrill. Right away I started plotting to insinuate a tree or two into a friend's apple orchard. I already knew that every Christmas from now on I would want medlars, soft cheese, dates and bread, friends in the living room, port in the wine glasses and a fire in the fireplace.

This did not convince me that medlars were dropped off the Christmas list because they were too sexy, even though I've since learned that the best way to eat one is to bite off the nipple at the stem end and suck out the flesh—admittedly a more carnal public act than eating a mandarin orange or a piece of fruitcake.

It seems more likely that medlars are an acquired taste, like olives, ripe cheeses, Scotch, and chili peppers, but one we've ceased to acquire. James Driver describes biting into a well-bletted medlar as a gourmet's delight: "Its extraordinary texture, that you suspect will prove repulsive, releases a fascinating spectrum of tastes. At first it is nutty, but then darker, earthier hints reminiscent of field mushrooms slip over the tongue, to leave an aftertaste as autumnal as a freshly picked Pippin."

Simin Tabrizi, who grew up in Tehran, came to see my medlars and show me how to eat them. As we sat at the table, sorting through them, weeding out ones that had grown mould at the calyx or had withered and hardened, and sampling the good ones, she told me that medlars, (*azgille* in Persian), were second only to pomegranates in her list of favourite fall fruits. My medlars weren't as sweet as the ones grown in Iran, and the fruit was squatter in shape, but they passed the test. From time to time she would eat another one, then sit back and say: "Oh. My goodness."

There's a medlar sitting on my desk right now, swollen and purple, shining under the lamp. I like to pick it up and look at the five-pointed star in the puckered flesh. You can read a pentagram as a human figure with outstretched arms and legs—a symbol of the microcosm or the integrated human being. Right side up, it's good luck. Turned upside down, it becomes the sign of black magic. Embedded in an open-erse, the pentagram has another layer of meaning. It suggests spirit embracing flesh, a joyful incarnation surrounded by the earthy electricity of blet.

Pheasant Under Glass

❧

SUPPOSE FOR A MOMENT THAT THERE WERE SUCH A THING AS an English-Food Dictionary. The translation for pheasant under glass would be: wealth, elegance, and exclusivity. You can get champagne at brunch in any medium-priced hotel. Caviar shows up in caviar pies at otherwise undistinguished buffets. Neither one holds a candle to pheasant under glass for evoking elegant and expensive dining.

Whisper the sibilant words to yourself: candlelight flickers over silver cutlery, wine sparkles in goblets, you sit at a formal dinner table surrounded by handsome men and pretty women wearing expensive clothes.

Pheasant under glass has its dark side, of course. Nothing stands better for nose-in-the-air waiters who sniff when displeased. Nothing conveys more clearly the essence of hoity-toity-ness, especially if you pronounce it "pheasant under gloss." And let us not forget that ever-droll slip of the tongue—peasant under glass.

How could we build such layers of meaning around a dish that most of us have never eaten? And once it reached the status of culinary icon, how could pheasant under glass disappear?

For pheasant under glass has disappeared. The only tables still graced by birds and glass domes are the ones we set in our minds.

It's no use stopping by Delmonico's after the theatre as fashionable people did in the 1890s, and ordering "a bird and a bottle"—pheasant under glass and a bottle of Bordeaux. They don't make it any more.

One thing you should know right now is that pheasant under glass is not a recipe, it's a presentation. The pheasant was generally roasted, but the seasonings were incidental. Trying to find a recipe for pheasant under glass is like looking for a recipe for hamburger in Styrofoam: it's a generic thing, served in a specific way. Serving pheasant under glass has at least two advantages. A glass dome keeps the heat in if the bird has to hold during the fish course. More important, when you lift the dome, the trapped odours burst like a blessing on the waiting senses. Pheasant under glass was not just a meal but a sensory occasion.

How it first came together at the dinner table is none too clear. Because pheasant under glass is not a recipe, you will not find it in recipe indexes. Current food dictionaries ignore it because it is passé. I suspect that writers of earlier dictionaries probably assumed that if you didn't already know how to serve pheasant under glass, you were better off not to try.

Here is the probable evolution of pheasant under glass according to Michael Batterberry, editor-in-chief and, with his wife Ariane, founder and co-publisher of the New York-based magazine, *Food Arts*: "Once the dinner party ground into full gear in the post-Civil War era, dinners became an occasion for conspicuous consumption. The older style of entertaining, a seated buffet, was replaced by service *á la Russe,* in which, ideally, there was one waiter for every guest. Pheasant under glass was a showpiece for that kind of meal. It was something done in grand hotels and in the mansions of the plutocrats."

By historical accident, the first food reporters arrived just as dinner parties entered this cycle of opulence. Women's magazines reported on what society hostesses served, and what they ate in restaurants. By 1910, everybody knew what a Waldorf salad was, and any cook with aspirations had made one. Pheasant under glass, equally celebrated, was out of reach of all but the wealthiest tables. Instead, it had unrestricted access to our imaginations, riding in on two shining ideas: pheasants and glass domes.

People have always thought highly of pheasants. The Greeks claimed that Jason and the Argonauts found them in Colchis, present-day Soviet Georgia, while looking for the Golden Fleece and brought them back as souvenirs. In the Middle Ages, you could swear on a pheasant. In the *Encyclopedia of Food*, Waverly Root tells us that Philip the Good, Duke of Burgundy, held a dinner in 1453 at which all the knights present swore by live pheasants—each pheasant tethered to a silver salver carried by a servant—that they would not rest until the Holy Land was recovered from the Infidel. Men with hawks went out to hunt pheasants; later, men with guns and dogs did the same. Pheasants imply hunting parties and large country houses, with money and leisure. Above all, pheasants are beautiful. See a pheasant picking its way through blond stubble—the brightest, most iridescent life in the landscape—and you won't soon forget it.

Glass domes share the smooth, glittering qualities of all glass and have, in addition, a more specific meaning: a world contained. It may be as brooding as Sylvia Plath's private hell in her novel *The Bell Jar* or as cheery as the little Christmas scene you shake to make the snow fall. No matter what's inside, the dome is the sky; it covers a world.

Pheasant under glass exists at that point in our minds where the idea of pheasant crosses the idea of glass domes. What happens is a sort of image explosion. Two strong ideas fuse. Pheasant under glass ceases to be food and becomes an icon. As food, pheasant under glass is a relic of a dead day. I'm not sorry. Excuse the pun, but pheasant under glass can't exist without a peasant under-class. Unless servants or waiters are plentiful and cheap, there is no such thing as pheasant under glass.

As an icon, it's going strong.

Gin:
The Crack of Its Day

EVEN IN THESE SOBER DAYS, IT IS HARD TO THINK OF SUMMER without thinking of gin and tonic. We may dither a little before we break down and buy the first bottle, the attendant six-pack of tonic water, and the limes. Who has time to drink cocktails any more? Life is too short for suffering the after-effects of drinks like the Pan Galactic Gargle Blaster in Douglas Adams' *The Hitch Hiker's Guide to the Galaxy*, an effect described as "having your brains smashed out by a slice of lemon wrapped round a large gold brick."

Despite our new moderation, we still drink gin and tonics, lured by the cool solace that enters in the wake of the first, bracingly bitter taste.

Gin and tonic conjures up tropical heat (Injah, you know), bare feet on shining teak floors, pith-helmeted officers in khakis, and sipping gin and tonic on the veranda at sunset as shadows deepen on the lawn and a scent of frangipani hangs in the warm air.

Why a reverie of the tropics should lie waiting in a bottle of gin is beyond my understanding. If anything, pouring a glass of gin ought to evoke a pale wraith, a shadowy woman clutching her bottle of gin-based patent medicine, the stuff jocularly known as Mother's Ruin.

Gin, after all, was the crack of its day. The youngest of the classic spirits, gin was a potent drug when it was first introduced, in the mid-sixteenth century. At 80 and 90 proof, it was five times as strong as the strongest fermented beer. And for a brief, very ugly period in British history, it was also cheap.

Gin was perfected at Holland's Leyden University by German physician and anatomist Franz de le Boë (Franciscus Sylvius), who was seeking a pleasant-tasting diuretic to be used as a blood-purifying tonic and a cure for gout. Like other chemists, Dr. Sylvius' basic ingredient was pure alcohol, distilled by the improved method developed by the eighth-century Arab alchemist Geber, and passed on to the Spanish during the Moorish conquest of Spain. Sylvius added juniper berries for their diuretic properties and other "botanicals," including coriander and angelica root, to the alcohol, then distilled the mixture again. He called it *genièvre*, the French word for juniper. The pleasantly bitter taste of juniper berries masked the roughness of the alcohol, and made a stimulating medicine that the Dutch, who shortened the name to geneva, came to believe was an indispensable tonic.

English soldiers first encountered geneva in Holland, in the course of the Thirty Years War, which finally ended in 1648. They shortened the name to gin, and brought home both the spirit and knowledge of the means to distill it.

At first gin kept its medicinal reputation. We know that Samuel Pepys drank "strong water of juniper" when he was feeling poorly, not when he wanted "merriment." British drink was beer or ale for the lower classes and French wines and brandies for those who could afford them. Then came a series of political decisions that set loose the destructive powers of the drink then known as Madame Geneva.

In 1689, the British Parliament invited Protestant William of Orange, the king of Holland, to remove his father-in-law, the unpopular Catholic King James II, from the throne. Along with William came William's fight with the French. Huge duties were imposed on French wines and brandies, effectively stopping trade. Then, in 1690, Parliament passed the Act for Encouraging the Distillation of Brandy and Spirits from Corn. The act was intended to give British farmers a market for their corn in times of good harvests, and so it did. All a budding distiller had to do was post a notice of intention to set up a still and wait ten days. And just for incentive, a tax was slapped on beer.

Gin, the drink of the Dutch court, was the obvious thing to make. Because it's flavoured by berries and herbs, gin can disguise the raw taste of inferior alcohol. It does not have to age. It is inexpensive to manufacture. In fact, most gin dealers didn't distill the spirit, they bought alcohol from the primary distillers, added oil of juniper and herbs—or, if they were unscrupulous, turpentine—and sold it.

Grocers sold it, chemists sold it, pubs, barbers, tobacconists, and madams sold it. Peddlers pushed carts loaded with jars of lethal gin and sold it by the glassful in the street. Signs appeared outside stables and sheds: "Drunk for 1d. Dead drunk for 2d. Straw for nothing." Gin drinkers lay on the straw, drinking, then passed out and slept it off. In 1730, London had more than seven thousand dram shops devoted to serving spirits—mostly gin.

Much like the urban poor in North American cities today, the poor of eighteenth-century London were displaced from farms by one of agriculture's recurring drives toward higher profits and fewer farm labourers. Rich, sweet, malt-brown Holland gin gave them temporary release from hunger and cold.

The eighteenth century had a forgiving attitude toward drink. The Pilgrim Fathers in Massachusetts brewed beer and corn liquor, and even the Quakers did not eschew alcohol until the 1770s. Alcohol was still considered medicinal, and beer qualified as a food. It wasn't until 1849, when Swedish physician Magnus Huss wrote a tract called *Alcoholismus chronicus,* that the world came to know the word "alcoholism." But the devastation wreaked by gin was so terrible that we can mark the beginnings of the modern temperance movement in the struggle against the manifest evils of gin.

William Hogarth's 1751 engraving "Gin Lane" is a vision of the substance-abuse section of Hell. A child falls to its death from its mother's arms, but mother is oblivious, passed out in a gin swoon. A suicide victim hangs in an upper-storey window, a man and wife pawn their saw and cooking pots to buy gin. A woman is being lifted into a coffin; her child lies on the ground, abandoned.

Hogarth was using artistic compression here, not exaggeration. The examples in real life were just as horrific. In 1734, a young woman called Judith Dufour was brought before the judges of the Old Bailey. She had strangled her two-year-old child, thrown its naked body into a ditch in Bethnal Green, then sold the clothes and used the money to buy gin. It's not for nothing that gin got its nickname—Mother's Ruin.

In the end, the interests of sobriety prevailed over the right of British farmers to find a ready market for their corn. Beginning in 1736, a series of acts were passed to restrict the distillation and sale of gin. At first the effects were a foreshadowing of the Prohibition era: more small-scale distillers producing an even more dangerous brew than before. In the end, heavy taxes on gin and lowered taxes on beer and ale forced gin upmarket, into the grandiose gin palaces of Dickens' day, where those who could afford it drank gin against a backdrop of gilt and mirrors.

Gin itself became lighter and more refined. With the invention of the continuous still, distillers began to make London Dry Gin, with less residue of the mash, less flavour, and less need to be sweetened. Gin lost its malt colour and became a pure, clear spirit. To taste what London's early gin drinkers tasted, you have to buy Dutch gin, also called Geneva, or Schiedam gin.

Gin's rehabilitation was furthered by a return to medicinal status, if only by association. British solders drank quinine water in the tropics to prevent malaria. By coincidence, nothing meshed as well with the flavour of quinine as gin.

And just as the apogee of gin drinking had given fuel to the beginnings of the temperance movement, the apogee of the temperance movement—Prohibition in the United States—brought enormous popularity to gin. Gin was the easiest illicit spirit to make: pure ethyl alcohol, obtained from a doctor under whatever medicinal pretext was necessary, mixed with juniper oil and other herbs, became "bathtub gin." At worst, bathtub gin could be lethal—a poison. At best it was rough to the taste, and couldn't be drunk without juice or soft drinks to hide the taste. The necessity to hide the taste of bad gin, in fact, might be considered the mother of the cocktail age. Beginning in the 1920s, a rage for mixed drinks brought increasingly more bizarre combinations, many of them decidedly feminine in nature: Pink Lady, White Lady, Gin Fizz, Cream Fizz, Grand Royal Fizz. For the morbidly curious, a Grand Royal Fizz is a jigger of gin, the juice of half a lemon, a half-tablespoon of powdered sugar, a dash of heavy cream, two dashes of maraschino liqueur, and the juice of half an orange. Mix it with ice in a cocktail shaker, pour it into a highball glass, add club soda, and garnish with fruit.

The cocktail era is as faded as the days when gin was a drunken guttersnipe. Gin is simply the summer drink now, at hand for times when it's necessary to visit the colonies without leaving home. Stored deep in the freezer, the summer's bottle of gin takes on a knife-sharp edge of smooth cold as it slowly empties. But the spirit of gin, a thin cool woman with a shady past, rises from every gin and tonic we pour. You can see her there, in her white summer dress, languidly chatting to the officers on the veranda.

Luwak Coffee

WE GLORIFY COFFEE, SUPPORT A COFFEE SHOP ON EVERY CORNER, and embrace caffeine as the last socially acceptable addiction. Even if we don't grind them ourselves, most of us have our favourite beans.

Surely, then, we might spare a moment, perhaps over a cup of coffee, to note that before they undergo more conventional processing, the world's most expensive coffee beans pass through the digestive tract of a small cat-like animal called a luwak. Officially it's *kopi luwak* (luwak coffee). Many of the people who sell it, at US$300 a pound, also call it "cat-poop coffee."

In Malaysia and Indonesia, where coffee connoisseurs drove up the price of luwak coffee centuries ago, the price of luwak coffee is explained like this: As fruit eaters, luwaks have an innate ability to pick the coffee cherries with the ripest and most juicy pulp. Logically, those cherries ought to hold at their centres the best beans. Those beans, partly fermenting as they travel through the luwak's digestive system, take on a layer of flavour that can't be duplicated and is worth paying for.

The North American market for luwak coffee is not there for the taste. We like our coffee to have a clear, clean flavour. According to specialty coffee merchant Michael Beach, owner of Raven's Brew Coffee in Ketchikan, Alaska, luwak coffee is "baggy, musty, earthy, and dirty, with no positive flavour characteristics." Others coffee merchants are more charitable. John Rotelli, broker and agent for L.J. Cooper Co. in Westchester, New York, which imports luwak coffee from Indonesia, says "it's a good cup of coffee, no doubt about it. It would fit industry standards. But I never quite got the real feeling inside of what makes it special."

My sense is that luwak coffee is special because it supplies comic relief with every cup. It's fun just saying the word: LOO-whack. Add to that the fact that anything to do with number two makes us giggle and you have a no-fail novelty item. The defecation jokes just go on and on.

At Raven's Brew, Beach talks to every prospective luwak coffee customer to make sure they understand it's "a crappy cup of coffee." For every quarter-pound order (US$75), he throws in a free T-shirt, with a cartoon luwak standing on a table, blinking at a few coffee cherries. A hand holds a coffee cup under the luwak's tail, a second hand reaches out to grab the tail and crank out a few more beans—straight from the luwak into the cup. For an animated version, as well as a comely photograph of a luwak, see <www.ravensbrew.com>.

Atlanta-based specialty coffee merchant John Martinez served luwak coffee at the 1995 Ig Nobel awards (for "individuals whose achievements cannot or should not be reproduced") after winning a prize in the nutrition category. To mark the occasion, he wrote an Ode to the Luwak, with the concluding couplet: "For all gathered here this is the scoop / We're drinking coffee from your poop."

Those of a gloomy temperament might take this scatological hilarity as just another confirmation of the rapidly approaching end of Western Civilization. We think of ourselves as connoisseurs, but our most expensive coffee bean owes its popularity to poop jokes.

I'd rather focus on the ray of hope that shines around every luwak coffee bean—a ray emanating from the unusual contract between humanity and a small, timid, fruit-loving carnivore. Humanity and its contracts with agricultural animals we know well enough. For most of us, the luwak is an unknown, even under its English name, palm civet.

The Latin is *Paradoxurus hermaphroditus*. The paradox is a tail that looks like it's prehensile, but isn't, although it can be slightly coiled at will. "Hermaphroditus" says nothing about the palm civet's anatomy, but speaks to all of those who ever had to rename a kitten due to the difficulty of determining the sex of carnivores.

Luwaks weigh between 1.5 and 4.5 kg. (3 to 10 pounds) and range from 43 to 70 cm (17 to 28 inches) in head and body length, with a tail of 40 to 66 cm (16 to 25 inches). They have a handsome coat pattern of longitudinal stripes on the back and spots on the shoulders, sides, and thighs, and sometimes at the base of the tail. In the jungle, they bed down in vines in the canopy, or failing that, a hole in a tree. Their preferred food is fruit, which has, over time, given them teeth less specialized for eating meat than most viverrids, the family of carnivores to which they, like mongooses and genets, belong.

To avoid predators, which include at least seven species of jungle cats, luwaks have become completely nocturnal. In a study conducted in Royal Chitwan National Park in Nepal, luwaks never came out before dark and always found shelter before dawn. They were busier on darker nights. On the four nights illuminated by a full moon, none of them left their resting trees. To picture luwaks at work, imagine a jungle night so dark that only the rustling sound from the top of the coffee trees tells us that they're feeding.

Most competitors for human crops are considered pests. Luwaks are "welcome members of the work force," according to the Friends of the National Zoo's web site <www.fonz.org/zoo­gooer/zg1996/luwak.htm>. By eating the fruity pulp that makes up 80 per cent of the coffee cherry's weight, they deliver the bean already processed, ready for washing, drying, and roasting.

We grow the coffee; they pick it, process it, and go to sleep. Without in any way disturbing them, we gather the beans from their scat and voila: something you can sell in Ketchikan, Alaska, for $75 for a quarter pound.

Search as I do, I can find no more equitable cross-species contract in the world of food production. It's nothing short of heartwarming.

The only worrisome note is the idea of a sudden luwak coffee boom, with luwak coffee showing up at every corner coffee bar. Luwaks produce such a small quality of coffee that a tad for it would mean one of two things, both nasty. Fraudulent claims to be selling luwak coffee would lead us to ask, with *Miami Herald* columnist Dave Barry: "What kind of world is this when you worry that people might be ripping you off by selling you coffee that was NOT pooped out by a weasel?"

Genuine luwak coffee in sudden abundance would, in its own way, be worse. It could only mean that we had found a way to break the most equitable contract people have ever made with an agricultural animal, and that somewhere, massive numbers of luwaks were being crammed into cages, as if they were so many laying hens. It would be enough to make you give up drinking coffee.

A Mess of Pottage

I WAS IN A BAPTIST CHURCH BASEMENT—UNDERGROUND, UNDER six, and under the influence of a Sunday-school teacher—when I first heard that Esau had sold his birthright for a "mess of pottage," whatever that might be. The moral was briskly drawn: don't trade something of great worth for something of little worth. We absorbed it as best we could and pressed on into the further mysteries of Genesis.

Like most Bible stories, it was a story I accepted as something that could only happen in some other world. My own experience of brothers was that they might tell you to look at that strange bird in the garden and then steal your piece of cake. They didn't generally try to sell you dinner for future considerations. Still, the "mess of pottage," that wonderful, rolling phrase, meant something to me. When I came across it in later reading it tasted, as it does still, more strongly of regret over a bad bargain than any other dish in English literature.

We may be stewing in our own juices, our goose may be cooked, our grand plans may turn, through some sad quirk of fate, to toast. Only a mess of pottage says so concisely that however hungry we may be, dinner wasn't worth what we paid.

Lately I've been wondering how an innocent dish of lentil stew came to have such sour associations. Here is something I learned on the way to finding out: stories that survive through the millennia are a bit like thorny roses. The meaning is likely to be live, and pointed. If you pick it up carelessly, it will prick your finger.

The story goes like this: Jacob and Esau were fraternal twins. Esau, the elder by a few seconds, was a hunter, a big, rough, red-headed man with a lot of body hair. Jacob was a shepherd. He was smaller, and not hairy. He stayed near the family tents, watching over the sheep.

One day Esau came back from hunting, skunked and hungry, and found Jacob boiling pottage. The account in the *New Oxford Annotated Bible* continues: "And Esau said to Jacob, 'Let me eat some of that red pottage, for I am famished!' Jacob said, 'First sell me your birthright.' Esau said, 'I am about to die; of what use is a birthright to me?'" and sealed the deal.

"Mess" originally meant serving. It is from the same Latin root that gives us the French word *mets*, for dish or viand. "Pottage" is an Anglicized version of *potage*, which in modern French means soup. In the seventeenth century it meant a big dish of meat or fish boiled with vegetables. "Porridge" is a word formed from pottage. In essence, it means nothing more specific than "something you boil in a pot."

The sixteenth-century translators who created the English Bible sometimes ate pottage with meat and vegetables in it. Sometimes their pottage was just stewed legumes, the cheap, sustaining food of the poor. As the rhyme "pease porridge hot, pease porridge cold, pease porridge in the pot, nine days old" tells us, a pottage sometimes overstayed its welcome.

The accepted belief is that Jacob's pottage was made of lentils. When Esau asks for some of Jacob's pottage, he calls it a "red pottage," and later, when he has agreed to sell his birthright for a meal, we read that "Jacob gave Esau bread and pottage of lentils, and he ate and drank, and rose and went on his way."

Certainly both Jacob and Esau were familiar with lentil stew. Lentils are one of the first plants humankind cultivated, nine thousand years ago when agriculture began. The dried seeds were portable, nutritious, and they kept well. Shepherds like Jacob ate stewed lentils and fed the stalks and foliage to nursing animals because they believed it increased milk yields.

There are two main kinds of lentils: red Egyptian lentils and brownish-grey lentils, also called French or European lentils. Red lentils have a more delicate flavour; French lentils are better known in North America. Either one might have been in Esau's pottage. Dean & DeLuca, grocers to New York's carriage trade, are clearly of the belief that it was the Egyptian red lentil that Esau ate. You can buy a 300-gram (10-ounce) bag of red lentils, wrapped in the famous label, bearing the pottage story on the back, for about five dollars. But Bible scholars believe that the word red doesn't refer to the lentils at all. Instead, it was an attempt to establish Esau as the father of the Edomites, a nomadic people who were enemies of the Israelites. In Hebrew, the words for red and for Edom are very similar.

This story was told by peasants living on the edge of the desert about the profligate ways of their nomadic neighbours. In political terms, Esau's bargain explained why Israel should rule over Edom: "It was because the Israelites, like their father Jacob, were cleverer, more provident and more self-controlled than the Edomites, represented by their father Esau," Cuthbert Simpson wrote in his exegesis on Genesis in the *Interpreter's Bible*.

We naturally identify with Jacob. It's his story, after all. Esau is a bit player. And besides, aren't we like Jacob—clever, provident, and self-controlled? We would never sell our birthright for cheap food.

It was at this point that the thorn pricked my thumb. In North America, we have the most efficient agricultural system in the history of the world. Monocultures on giant farms, fertilizers, and pesticides have allowed us to grow more food for more people at a lower dollar price than any society that preceded us. In other words, cheap food.

Our birthright as North Americans is virgin soil. We live on a continent of amazing fertility, a continent that has never had to support large human populations. After fifty years of modern chemical agriculture, the organic content of prairie soils has declined to 36 from 49 per cent. Fertilizers and pesticides are showing up in plankton in the Arctic Ocean. The U.S. loses three billion tonnes of soil to erosion every year. The Prairies are blowing away

Yet we still buy our groceries believing that it's always better to spend less on food. We don't even have a currency for measuring the cost to the earth. If every food we bought were tagged with its ecological price as well as its price in dollars, the scandalous figures that usually accompany the words "organically grown" would look reasonable by comparison.

You want people who are primitive and heedless of the future? Try us.

At least Esau knew enough to be sorry. I like to think of him knocking around eternity, muttering: "You don't know what you've got until it's gone."

I suspect this recipe bears no relationship at all to the dish of lentils that Esau ate. For one thing, I like to use du Puy lentils, for their lovely green colour and for their ability to keep their shape when cooked. For another, Esau never ate a sweet potato—it's a new-world food.

This is less a soup than a stew, thick and dry enough to roll up in filo pastry and bake if you're looking for a vegetarian main course. On less formal occasions, I serve it with rice, yogurt on the side, and a simply cooked green vegetable—steamed green beans flash-fried in oil, grated ginger, and salt, for example. Asafetida added to the lentils as they cook will reduce their gassy tendencies.

Curried Lentils and Sweet Potatoes

1 cup (250 mL) du Puy lentils
1 tsp. (5 mL) green cardamom pods, about 15
generous pinch of asafetida (optional)
1 Tbsp. (15 mL) butter
1 Tbsp. (15 mL) vegetable oil
1½ Tbsp. (22 mL) finely chopped ginger
2 Tbsp. (30 mL) finely chopped jalapeño pepper
1 tsp. (5 mL) whole cumin seed
1 tsp. (5 mL) black mustard seed
1 lb. (500 g) sweet potatoes, peeled and diced
1 cup (250 mL) vegetable stock
1 tsp. (5 mL) brown sugar
1 tsp. (5 mL) salt
4 Tbsp. (60 mL) finely chopped cilantro, divided
juice of one lemon

Heat the lentils in cold water with the cardamom and asafetida. Bring to a boil and cook 20 minutes, or until the lentils are soft.

In a large frying pan, heat the oil and butter. Add the ginger, jalapeño, cumin, and black mustard seed. Stir and fry for a moment or two, until the mustard seeds begin to pop.

Add the diced sweet potatoes and cook, stirring, for five minutes. Add the stock, brown sugar, salt, and half of the cilantro. Cover and let cook for 10 minutes, or until the sweet potato is tender.

Uncover and cook until any excess liquid evaporates. Squeeze the lemon over the lentils and sprinkle on the remaining cilantro.

Serves four.

REAL MARSMALLOWS
AND OTHER PARADOXES
OF MODERN FOOD

Cotton Candy

IS THERE A MORE SATISFYING PIECE OF MAGIC AT A FALL FAIR than watching a teenager in a booth grab a paper cone and expertly, almost instantly, wrap your cotton candy around it? The fact that cotton candy is, furthermore, messy, sticky, capable of getting entangled in your sister's hair, sweet, pliable, and able to be compressed into tiny bits by the pressure of your fingers, is just icing.

Cotton candy is sugar pressed to startling extremes by physical force. A cotton-candy machine consists of a metal head mounted in the centre of a tub. The head holds the sugar. Electrical elements that look a lot like an elastic metal watchband wrap the sugar container and heat the sugar to 120°F (40°C), a temperature at which it will melt but not caramelize. When the machine is turned on, the head spins at 3,600 rpm. Centrifugal force presses the melted sugar past the heating elements and out of the head through slits in the metal casing. Hot, liquid sugar hits the outside air like a bucket of water being hurled into a flash-freezer. In a millisecond it crystallizes into sugar ice.

Because the molten sugar is travelling so fast, the sugar crystals form into long, thin threads, so thin that a thousand together are as soft as snow, or sugar wool (*Zuckerwolle*) as the Germans would have it, or Dad's beard (*barbe de Papa*), according to the French. The "floss" of British and Canadian "candy floss" may come from a French word meaning soft or downy, or it may be a native English or Scandinavian word related to fleece.

A stick of cotton candy is a pink or blue bubble, a delicate, temporary sweetness, brought to you by the elemental powers of the fairground: heat and centrifugal force.

Cotton candy was, naturally enough, introduced to the world at a fair—the Louisiana Purchase Exposition of 1904, in St. Louis, Mississippi. Called Fairy Floss, it was made in the new "electric candy machine," patented by William Morrison and John Wharton, owners of the Electric Candy Company of New York and Nashville. You got a box of it, the size of a box of current-day Cracker Jack, for 25 cents. The edifying experience of watching it being made was free.

Admission to the fair was 50 cents; you could buy a man's shirt for 25. But even at 25 cents, fairy floss was a hit—68,655 people shelled out their quarters for threads of spun sugar. If I'd been there and had a quarter, I'd have bought it too. Cotton candy is a genuinely exciting food with only two drawbacks: it has no food value beyond calories, and it tastes like what it is—sugar. Children were, and remain, delighted.

Cotton-candy machines spread rapidly through the United States and to Europe, suffering technological regression as they spread. Morrison and Wharton found themselves holding a patent that was several years ahead of its time, because it was several years ahead of widely available electricity. Competitors found it easier to sell flame-heated, hand-cranked machines. Electricity won out eventually, of course. It seems Morrison and Wharton didn't profit greatly from their invention. The Electric Candy Company split in two shortly after 1904; neither company survives.

Modern machines produce more floss faster than the first machines, but are in essence the same. You can buy a Mini-floss stand that turns out two a minute, for $1,000, or a Tornado Floss machine, that will give you eight a minute for $2,000. Gold Medal Products Company of Cincinnati, Ohio, the largest, and until recently, the only North American manufacturer of cotton-candy machines, makes both of them.

Cotton-candy technology has not entirely stood still, of course. Modern cotton candy is coloured and flavoured by Flossine, an artificially coloured and flavoured powder which is also sold by Gold Medal. One heaping tablespoon of Flossine will flavour and colour five pounds of sugar: lemon yellow, lime green, blue raspberry, pink bubble gum, and more.

An even more disconcerting evolution is cotton candy sold in plastic bags. Packaged that way, and unopened, it will keep for seven to ten days, although I can't imagine why anyone would want to eat cotton candy ten days removed from the fair. The big draw for floss in a bag is tidiness. Small children are more likely to eat it and less likely to wear it than floss on a stick.

Since children, immediacy, and magic are central to the success of cotton candy, you might be tempted to think that cotton candy in a plastic bag is a travesty. But I recently saw a toddler coming out of the poultry barn at the Pacific National Exhibition in Vancouver with a bag of cotton candy. She pulled off a patch between two fingers, and ate it with a dreamy, far-gone look on her face. As far as I could tell, she was in no way impeded in her experience of the manna of a fair.

Given the ease of making cotton candy, and the profit margin involved in selling an ounce of coloured sugar for about $1.50, it's surprising that in North America at least, cotton candy has stayed firmly associated with fairs. Other fair foods—iced tea and ice cream cones, for example, both introduced in 1904 at St. Louis— have leapt the fairground fence and escaped into day-to-day eating. Jack Hunter, who's been selling cotton candy at fairs since the 1940s, told me you can't sell cotton candy in a mall because no one buys it. Pete Bally, northwest regional manager for Gold Medal, says cotton candy "has really taken off" in video rental stores. I'm not convinced it will transplant successfully. Malls and video stores are places of steady, mercantile coldness. Cotton candy demands heat and centrifugal force.

A fair's heat is the heat of late summer, the stored sun burning inside the biggest pumpkin, and the fattest hog. It's the heat of crowds too, a heat that used to burn hotter back when fair-goers spent the year with a limited number of human faces—just the family and whomever lived in a radius of ten miles from the farm.

Fairs are places where you see strange people, some of them simply strangers, some of them sword swallowers or bearded ladies. Fairs exist at the edges of the possible. Eggs might hatch into chickens while you watch. There could be a two-headed calf or, as there was in St. Louis, Jim Key—"The Most Wonderful Horse in the World"—who read, wrote, counted, and gave change. It's enough to make your head spin, and if it doesn't, you can always enlist the help of the roller coaster or the Tilt-a-Whirl.

Can there possibly be a truer parallel to a fair than cotton candy?

Fairs are places where you pay money on a hot day to travel through space at high speed, with centrifugal force pressed like a big hand against your chest until your nerves spin out in long, fine threads.

Ketchup

IF WE'RE TO BELIEVE THE STATISTICS, KETCHUP IS THE MOST popular condiment in North America. Yes, the dollar value of salsa exceeds that of ketchup, but salsa is more expensive. By volume, ketchup still rules.

That means ketchup is one of the shaping flavours of our cuisine, the equivalent of soy sauce in Japan, or fish sauce in Thailand. It's what most North Americans choose to taste, most of the time.

So what is the true taste of ketchup?

While it may not have the same cachet as "what is the sound of one hand clapping?" this is a koan worth pursuing. Ketchup is our defining sauce. It is also alone among condiments in having no widely available high-quality form. In their respective cuisines, soy sauce and fish sauce can be had in varying grades, and at their best, belong on the most refined tables. Ketchup is never found in upscale restaurants, and comes, for all but a few of us, in one grade: industrial.

And as the Reagan administration found out in 1981, when it tried to save money on school lunch programs by classifying ketchup as a vegetable, our *sauce du pays* is, in fact, roundly despised. The idea that a hamburger patty with ketchup could count as one meat and one vegetable serving set off a furious reaction. Ray Sokolov speculates in his book *Why We Eat What We Eat* that even if the amount of ketchup a third grader used on fries was the nutritional equivalent of a whole tomato, the anti-ketchup forces would not have been mollified, since ketchup was "tainted by its connection with fast food." In fact, the function of ketchup in North American life is to draw a line between food you can safely eat as a steady diet, and food you can't.

Yet if we are what we eat, and the condiment we eat most is unacceptable, what does that make us? And why are we content to believe that wholesome food isn't as good tasting or as much fun as the food we eat with ketchup?

My tussle with the ketchup koan began when a friend offered me some homemade ketchup to taste. She had discovered an almost empty bottle in the fridge, just before sitting three kids down to a veggie-burger supper. So, "because it was easier than going to the store," she made ketchup.

The recipe my friend used was a low-sodium ketchup from Anne Lindsay's *The Lighthearted Cookbook*. Other ketchup recipes that I had read, and quickly cast aside, involved peeling and seeding a whole lot of tomatoes and then cooking them for a long time, with plenty of chances to scorch the tomatoes and ruin the batch. This one started with a can of tomato paste, which is exactly how Heinz starts, only on a larger scale. You put the tomato paste in a jar, add a number of common household ingredients—water, vinegar, sugar, and spices—then shake well. It keeps, covered, for a month in the fridge.

I went home and, in less than five minutes, made my own ketchup, without even assembling the ingredients before I started timing myself.

It tasted close enough to my memory of ketchup that I thought it could pass as the real thing, as long as you put it in a Heinz bottle and didn't tell. Seized by a spirit of scientific inquiry, I set out three bowls: one held my ketchup, one Heinz's and the third, Larry Forgione's American Spoon Brand Smoky Ketchup.

Larry's was good, but too smoky to qualify as real ketchup. Mine tasted like ketchup, with a strong tomato flavour. The real shocker was Heinz out of a bottle, the ur ketchup. It had two poles of flavour, one sweet and one sour, and in between, where you might expect to taste tomato, lay a vast emptiness, with a faint overtone of—what?

The Heinz label lists tomato paste, white vinegar, liquid sugar, fructose syrup, salt, onion powder, and spices. No help there. For a few unsteady moments it seemed possible that Garrison Keillor's Ketchup Advisory Board skits (available at <www.npr.org>) were not absurdist melodrama after all. The board is a fictional sponsor of Minnesota Public Radio's show called *A Prairie Home Companion*. Each week's "commercial" features Barb and Jim, middle-aged Middle Americans who are supposed to be enjoying "the good years." After all, "the kids have dropped out of their cult so we no longer run into them at the airport" and "that funny smell wasn't from either one of us; it was a dead squirrel in the furnace."

Every week Barb and Jim face a dilemma. His application to The Famous Decorators School is rejected, with a note calling his work "puerile and jejune." She steps on the scale in their hotel room and finds out how much she really weighs. Each week they turn to ketchup for comfort, because "ketchup has natural mellowing agents," that "help a person through the little crises," or "help dull the pain of unrealized dreams," or "make a person feel like you're full of endorphins, even if you're not."

A more likely explanation of what ketchup tastes like and why it tastes that way comes from Andrew F. Smith's 1996 book, *Pure Ketchup: A History of America's National Condiment, with Recipes*. As Smith explains it, ketchups had been popular long before the 1860s, when the first commercial tomato ketchups were sold. Early ketchups were made from walnuts, mushrooms, oysters, mussels, beef liver, plums, whortleberries, and almost anything else you'd care to mention, except tomatoes, a new-world fruit unknown to Europeans until the seventeenth century, and widely feared as poisonous for two hundred years after that.

By 1900, several types of tomato ketchup were on the market, including thin, fermented ketchups and sour ketchups. They flavoured soups, gravies, sauces, and salad dressings, and were used as a condiment with steak, chops, roasts, cutlets, fish, oysters, and eggs.

Tomato ketchup was inexpensive to make and wildly popular. In 1907 Henry J. Heinz pumped more than 12 million bottles out of the world's largest ketchup factory.

Early makers of quality ketchups, including Heinz, started with ripe tomatoes. Ketchup could also be made as a highly profitable by-product of tomato processing. "Tomato canneries discarded small, irregularly shaped, green, or rotten fruit," Smith writes. "Ripe, red tomatoes were skinned, pared and cored. Rotten and diseased sections, worm and insect holes, and green and unripe hard parts were cut out. These rejected pieces and fruits—otherwise referred to as trimmings, refuse, waste, or slop—were tossed onto the floor of the cannery. Trenches collected the trimmings and juice that gushed from the tomatoes as they were prepared for canning. These trenches were scraped out and the refuse was swept off the floor. Both were dumped into barrels…" —which were then sold to ketchup makers, who added coal dyes for colour and borax, boric acid, and salicylic acid, all of them hazardous to human health, as preservatives.

It's at this point in the story that we meet Arvil and Katherine Bitting, First Couple of Ketchup. Their professional and personal partnership lasted more than forty years and changed the taste of ketchup forever. Katherine, née Golden, studied microbiology at MIT in the early 1890s. She met and married Arvil, then a professor of veterinary medicine, while she was teaching at Purdue University.

By 1907, Katherine and Arvil were both working for the U.S. Department of Agriculture. Their project: a preservative-free ketchup. The Bittings inspected ketchup factories and watched home ketchup makers at work with traditional recipes—none of which called for preservatives aside from vinegar and salt. They set up a lab in their house and tested 1,600 bottles of commercially made ketchup. Eventually they published two monographs,

Arvil's "Ketchup: Methods of Manufacture," and Katherine's "Microscopic Examination," bound together as one volume.

The Bittings proved that manufacturers who started with wholesome ingredients and kept them clean didn't need preservatives. All they had to do was store the pulp in airtight tin containers, not wooden barrels; sterilize it by cooking it at high temperatures; use more vinegar; and increase the percentage of tomato solids. The result was thicker ketchup with a much stronger taste of vinegar and sugar. Unfortunately, the chemicals that give tomatoes their flavour turned out to be susceptible to heat; both germs and tomato flavour perished together.

With the best of intentions, the Bittings had introduced the defining taste of industrial food—safety achieved at the cost of flavour.

After some experimenting with recipes, this is my favourite version of fast ketchup. It's based on the recipe for Homemade Ketchup in Anne Lindsay's Lighthearted Cookbook, *but is more peppery and less sweet.*

Faster Than Going to the Store Ketchup

1 $5\frac{1}{2}$-oz. (156-mL) can tomato paste
3 Tbsp. (45 mL) packed brown sugar
$\frac{1}{4}$ cup (50 mL) water
2 Tbsp. (30 mL) cider vinegar
$\frac{1}{2}$ tsp. (2 mL) Dijon mustard
$\frac{1}{4}$ tsp. (1 mL) cinnamon
$\frac{1}{8}$ tsp. (0.5 mL) finely ground black pepper
pinch each, cloves and allspice

In a jar or bowl, combine all the ingredients and stir well. Cover and store in the refrigerator for up to one month.

Makes 1 cup (250 mL).

Cheezies

EVERY INVENTION STARTS WITH A QUESTION. GRASP A LIGHT bulb or turn on a garden hose, and you are handling the answer to someone's puzzle. Some of these questions are easy enough to intuit from the objects they give birth to; others are more obscure. Safety pins are an open book—how do I keep a diaper on my child without stabbing incidents? So are canned peas—how can we save these for later? And recorded music—how can we hear this again?

But what question do you have to ask in order to have the answer be Cheezies?

I can tell you right away not to bother looking in the realms of gastronomy, or nutrition, or philosophy. It's a physics question, and here is its most basic form: What will happen if I heat a glutinous cereal starch under pressure and then suddenly release the pressure?

The man who first framed the question is Alexander P. Anderson, the father of puffed cereals. Anderson was working in a laboratory in New York in 1901 when he heated starch in a sealed test tube and then broke the tube. The result was a white, puffy foam, crunchy to bite into, but yielding.

Here is what had happened inside the test tube. Moisture in the starch had turned to steam, and the steam pushed against the walls of the test tube. When Anderson broke the test tube, steam rushed out, pulling hot starch molecules with it. The starch had been puffed full of air. At the cost of a broken test tube, humanity had succeeded in duplicating what God did in order to make popcorn.

Anderson tackled the next question—how can I use this discovery to make money?—by teaming up with The Quaker Oats Company in Chicago to develop the world's first puffing guns for cereals. In 1904, the crowd at the St. Louis world fair had its first taste of puffed rice, which was sold as a popcorn-like snack. It was not a great success until the next year, when Anderson and Quaker Oats realized that although they had duplicated the process that makes popcorn, the product they had to sell was actually a breakfast cereal.

The supplementary question that evoked Cheezies was slightly more specific. Before we discuss it, I had better be clear here that when I write "Cheezies," I mean Hawkins' Cheezies, and no others. Hawkins has the trademark on the name. The careless may call any cheese-flavoured exploded starch snack a "cheesie," just as we say Kleenex instead of facial tissue, but people who eat them know that there is only one Cheezie: that produced by W.T. Hawkins Ltd., made in Belleville, Ontario.

Hawkins' have heft; the others are full of air. Hawkins' taste better. There is no chemical tang at the end, just a giant salt rush. Other cheese-flavoured exploded starch products are as dry as the Sahara and as rough as steel wool in the mouth. Cheezies are velvet on first touch, then they become crunchy. Most important of all, Hawkins Cheezies, despite being a food of the machine age, have escaped uniformity. "Every Cheezie is different," says Shirley Woodcox, manager of the W.T. Hawkins plant, "they're like snowflakes and people." I don't know if I'd go that far, but the diverse shapes of Hawkins' do make other cheese-flavoured exploded starch snacks look like so many fluorescent orange worm larvae.

To return to our question: the inventor who posed the specific query that resulted in Hawkins' Cheezies was an Ohio machinist called Jim Marker. For him, it was a mechanical question with gastronomic overtones: How do you make long, salty, cheese-flavoured fingers out of exploded corn?

The time was just after the Second World War. The company Marker worked for was one of hundreds searching the wide-open field of processed food, looking for another ticket to wealth, like corn flakes or shredded wheat. W.T. Hawkins bought the company Marker worked for and moved Marker to Chicago. There, with a handful of machine shops at his beck and call, Marker made the minute adjustments that resulted in the Cheezie.

He was working blind because the action was hidden inside the walls of the puffing gun. It was a matter of tinkering and seeing what resulted, then going back to tinker some more. "You are doing things you can't see," Marker says. At last he hit the modification that made Cheezies. All that remained was to spray the cornmeal fingers with melted cheddar in big rotating cylinders.

As the Chicago plant prospered, Hawkins sent Marker, a mere sprat of 27, off to open a plant in Canada. Four years later, in 1953, the Hawkins Chicago plant closed and the true Cheezie became as Canadian as the Maple Leaf.

At 82, Marker is vice-president of W.T. Hawkins and still at work, tasting each batch of Cheezies to make sure it's faithful to the Hawkins formula. He has, as you might imagine, a fondness for cheese. Before he goes to bed at night he puts a block of cheddar and some soda crackers on his bedside table. If he wakes up hungry, he eats a wedge of cheddar and finishes it off with a few soda crackers. "I like salt," he says.

So do we, Mr. Marker. So do we. And so we reach a philosophical question: Can any Cheezie, even a Hawkins Cheezie, be good?

Cheezies are junk food, snack food, the sort of food the snack food industry piously tells us to eat only when we've already had our three squares. No rational meal includes Cheezies. Hawkins prints a recipe for a Cheezies dip on the back of the package; in the freewheeling '60s, there were recipes calling for crushed Cheezies as a casserole topping, but this is just show. Cheezies are their own event. Nothing but Coke truly complements their violent colour and aggressively salty taste.

The two things that make them irrevocably junk food are these: they will be eaten in whatever quantity is available, and they will provoke guilt. First the gastronomic guilt Cheezies short out the palate, and for days afterwards nothing tastes salty enough. Nutritional guilt follows. Like most processed foods, a bag of Cheezies manages to be less than the sum of its parts. Cornmeal and cheddar cheese are nutritious foods, even if cheese is fatty enough to be in the borderline category of things you shouldn't eat too often. The cornmeal fingers in Cheezies are deep-fried before they meet the cheese, sending the fat level even higher.

Down at the very bottom of the Cheezies bag there's another bit of guilt, a harder one to see clearly. It might be the guilt that attends on the sin of pride. We have, after all, made the Almighty look rather small with that popcorn trick of His. We shoot off guns that bellow and roar; His exploded starch snack can be contained in any saucepan with a lid.

And it might be a gnawing awareness that there's something very strange about exploding cereals before we eat them, making them simultaneously less nutritious and more expensive in the process.

Suppose, tomorrow morning, we were all to come to our right minds for just one moment. Suppose we saw clearly that there can't be peace on earth, or ecological survival, until we establish a rational way to distribute food on this small planet of ours, and asked a question. We all know that the answer wouldn't be Cheezies.

Twinkies

WHEN THE ONLY SNACK CAKE EVER CONVICTED OF INCITING A double murder turns 70, you have to stop and take a look.

The Twinkie officially left its sixties behind on April 6, 2000, with not much more to mark the date than a special birthday wrapper, featuring "Twinkie the Kid," an animated Twinkie wearing a Stetson and cowboy boots, lassoing lit candles off a birthday cake. (Check the Twinkies web site, <www.twinkies.com>, to view it.)

The Kid, a mere 29 years old as a cartoon character, looks cheerful—more cheerful, in fact, than the Twinkie itself. And fair enough. Not every birthday is a happy one, especially when the celebrant has already served 21 years of a life sentence of public ridicule.

A Twinkie, for anyone unclear on this, is a single-portion sponge cake, longer than it is wide, with a "creamy" (not cream) filling, sold in a plastic sleeve. If you flip a Twinkle on its back you will see the three holes where mechanical nipples squirted the filling into the cake.

But a Twinkie is much more than a mere cake. It's a live cultural presence, a symbol of all junk food, signifying everything packaged and false. So, in an *American Spectator* article titled "Dark Women Rule," writer Stephen Chapman, arguing that a natural blonde is as rare as an albino rhinoceros, adds: "If you are prepared to settle for technologically engineered beauty—breast implants, nose jobs, facelifts, liposuction, fake eyelashes and tinted contact lenses—then, by all means, blondes are for you. So, probably, are Hostess Twinkies."

The Dictionary of American Slang adds that a twinkie is "a young, sexually attractive person," especially a teenager or homosexual. Presumably Archie Bunker wasn't aware of that last association when he called Twinkies "WASP soul food," and demanded them for his lunch bucket.

Even those who aren't sure if a Twinkie is chocolate (it isn't; that chocolate thing you ate is probably a cupcake or a Ding Dong) are sure that the Twinkie's nutritional value is on the negative side of the scale. The consensus: in all but the most extraordinary circumstances, you'd be better off not eating it.

Jim Dewar, father of the Twinkie, ate either several a day, or at least two packages a week, depending on which account you prefer. "Some people say Twinkies are the quintessential junk food, but I believe in the things," he told an interviewer. "I fed them to my four kids, and they feed them to my fifteen grandchildren."

Dewar started his career in 1920 as a delivery boy for Continental Bakery of Chicago, selling pound cake from a horse-drawn wagon. In 1930, he was plant manager, on the lookout for what he called "a good two-pack nickel number."

He decided to use the little loaf pans used to make sponge-cake bases for strawberry shortcakes, which sat empty when it wasn't strawberry season, and fill them with something creamy. In itself, the idea of a pastry filled with cream is not new. Sugar doughnuts filled with Bavarian cream operate on a similar principle. The stroke of genius came on a business trip to St. Louis, where Dewar saw a billboard of an enormous pair of shoes, and stumbled on "the best darn-tootin' idea I ever had."

Did the shoes somehow remind him of his little cream-filled cakes? Certainly the copy, "Twinkle-Toe Shoes," struck latent gold in his mind, and he named his new snack cake Twinkies.

There could not be a better name for a snack cake. "Twinkie" is reminiscent of "wink," the most conspiratorial of all human gestures, and of "twinkle," the friendliest kind of light there is. Loving people's eyes twinkle, and so does a light in a window, seen through the dark from a few miles away.

The Twinkie was an immediate success. Marketed nationally along with Wonder Bread, another of Continental's major lines, it entered a time of happy celebrity that peaked in the 1950s. Twinkies were, in fact, proud sponsors of the first hit children's television program, *The Howdy Doody Show*. Every weekday afternoon at Howdy Doody time, millions of children sat and gaped as Howdy and his grown-up friend, Buffalo Bob, talked about how much they liked Twinkies. Twinkies were "Howdy Doody's favourite petit four," Jane and Michael Stern write in their *Encyclopedia of Bad Taste*. There was even an early version of Twinkie the Kid, a cowhand who lived in Doodyville.

Kids loved Twinkies and Twinkies loved kids. Mothers tucked Twinkies into their children's lunches, one convenient, individually wrapped snack cake in each brown paper bag, along with the apple and the sandwich.

But in November 1978, when Dan White killed San Francisco mayor George Moscone and Harvey Milk, the city's first openly gay supervisor, everything fell apart. White, a former police officer, was elected a San Francisco supervisor, then resigned because the pay was too low. When his parents offered to supplement his income, White asked for his job back. After Mayor Moscone refused to rescind the resignation, White entered the city hall through a basement window, killed the mayor, and then walked down the hall to Milk's office and killed him.

White pleaded not guilty to charges of first-degree murder. He admitted shooting Milk and Moscone, but said he wasn't responsible because he had been eating a diet of Coca-Cola, cupcakes, chocolate bars, and Twinkies, and the ill effects of that diet on his body chemistry intensified his existing depression. The sugar made him do it.

"The Twinkie Defense," as the argument instantly came to be called, worked. White was convicted on the reduced charge of voluntary manslaughter and served less than six years. He was released from prison in January 1985, and committed suicide eight months later.

The Twinkie itself had not, officially, been on trial. But when White was convicted on reduced charges, some of the blame stuck to the snack cake.

Dan White ate chocolate bars and cupcakes, and washed them down with Coke. But no one talked about the Mars Bar defence, or the Coke defence.

The Twinkie, once a cream-filled sponge cake that mothers could happily tuck into their children's lunches, had turned into the Anti-Food, a substance so negative in its effects on the body that, if eaten in quantity, it could impair your mind and lead you to violence. What could be more natural then, than the 1994 testimony of James W. Johnston, CEO of R.J. Reynolds Tobacco Co., that tobacco "is no more addictive than coffee, tea, or Twinkies"?

As the Twinkie enters its eighth decade, alarms about junk food are going off again. In fact, the birthday fell uncomfortably close to a devastating article, "Let Them Eat Fat," that appeared in the March 2000 *Harpers*. Author Greg Critser examines what he calls "the deadly fattening of our youth." Critser estimates that "the cost [of obesity] to the general public health budget by 2020 will run into the hundreds of billions, making HIV look, economically, like a bad case of the flu."

It works like this: after supersized meals of burgers, fries, and soft drinks, sugar and fat bombard the pancreas, eventually wearing out its insulin-producing "islets." Next comes diabetes and what Critser calls "its inevitable dirge of woes: kidney, eye, and nerve damage; increased risk of heart disease; even stroke."

In response to this gathering catastrophe, Eli Lilly, the drug company, is building the largest single-drug factory ever built, devoted to insulin. So clear is the rising tide of obesity, so well-known the medical consequences, that, as ghoulish as it might seem, any pharmaceutical companies ignoring this burgeoning market are, Critser writes, "bordering on fiduciary mismanagement."

Sugar itself belongs on the list of legal drugs, along with alcohol, tobacco, and caffeine, because it follows "the habituation paradigm," says Harvard-trained epidemiologist John Newmeyer. "You eat some, it makes you feel good right away. A few hours later, the effects wear off. You feel not so good again, so you want more of it to restore the good feeling."

Per capita consumption of sugar has grown approximately 20 per cent, from 127 pounds in 1986 to 156 pounds in 1998, making it, Newmeyer says, "the real success story of legal drugs in the past twenty years."

Newmeyer, who specializes in HIV and substance abuse epidemiology at the Haight Ashbury Free Clinic in San Francisco, believes that by focusing on the dangers of illegal drugs, "we are looking for the mouse that is gnawing away at the baseboards. Meanwhile, the unacknowledged elephants in the room—alcohol, caffeine, tobacco and sugar—are wrecking the house." Once again, the Twinkie, as the representative of all junk food, stands accused. But this time the blame is even more unfair.

Twinkie offers lots of fat and sugar, but you could halt Twinkie production entirely and the effect on North American obesity would be nil. According to "Nutrition News Focus," an electronic newsletter, "soft drinks are the number two source of carbohydrates, behind bread, in diets of the typical American child and adult." And those soft drinks now come in enormous quantities. "When I was growing up, a Coke was seven ounces," Newmeyer says. "Now they're 20 ounces, and a supersized Coke is 42 fluid ounces and refillable."

Who could blame the Twinkie, if, leaning over to blow out the candles, its birthday wish is: "This time, please let them pin it on Coke."

Real Marshmallows

NO FOOD IS AS BELOVED IN PRINCIPLE AND LOATHED IN PRACTICE as the marshmallow.

Friends of a friend, on their way to a week of cottage camping, stopped to pick up the makings for the campfire classic, s'mores. The marshmallows, graham wafers, and chocolate were assembled on the counter when one of them said: "You know, I don't really like these."

"Oh," said the other. "Neither do I." So they put them back on the shelves.

We all know that it wasn't the graham wafers or the chocolate that tipped the scales. Sure, marshmallows are fun to roast around a campfire—at least until your big brother lights his on fire and, waving it around to put it out, dislodges it from its pointed stick and sends it sailing through the air to land, still in flames, on your hand.

Marshmallows are cute. They're squishy. They have a fascinating texture. But they're fake, a food of the dark side, nutritionally negative, gastronomically appalling, a byword for the worst excesses of 1950s processed food. If there were a culinary division of crimes against humanity, marshmallows would be behind bars, along with Cool Whip, Miracle Whip, Jell-O, Minute Rice, and canned pineapple—all guilty of taking part in the twentieth century's most heinous recipe, the marshmallow salad.

This is why "real marshmallows" sounds like an oxymoron. But there is such a thing, made from the ground root of the marshmallow plant. *Althaea officionalis* looks like a shorter, bushier version of a hollyhock, with similar, but smaller, flowers. There's a cluster of them growing in the herb garden on the third-floor deck of Vancouver's Fairmont Waterfront Hotel, which is how executive chef Daryle Nagata came to be serving marshmallows in the hotel's restaurant, Herons—not normally a marshmallow-friendly zone.

Nagata's marshmallows are arranged in a campfire scene on a wooden platter, with a tea-light standing in for the campfire. They come in four flavours: yellow is saffron and bee pollen, white is vanilla and coconut milk, pink is rosehips and candied ginger, and green is bee balm and lemon verbena. The colours are pastel, the flavours muted; the shape is a cube with squared-off edges, not the classic scale model of a toilet paper roll. They are more fragile than commercial marshmallows. Pick one up in the middle and the edges will start to droop. There's no discernable marshmallow taste, but there's no chemical after-burn either. You can eat four in rapid succession and not get a sugar headache.

Here's the best thing about marshmallows made from real marshmallow: they let us reunite the marshmallow of the green, living world with marshmallow candy. With real marshmallows, we get to reconnect something that's been severed for at least 130 years.

Nagata made his marshmallows using an infusion of the dried roots, which is roughly the same way they were first made, by Parisian confectioners, at the beginning of the nineteenth century. At the time, the confectioner was part pharmacist, charged with making prescriptions better tasting by adding sugar or honey. Confectioners often worked with marshmallow. As far back as the fourth century BCE it was used in cough medicine because it coats the tissues in the throat and soothes them.

Marshmallow still has a loyal following among herbalists. Nagata's gardening partner, master gardener and clinical herbalist Elaine Stevens, says: "*Officionalis* in the name means that marshmallow has official healing status. In the Middle Ages, it was grown all over Europe in monastery gardens. "The flowers are good for skin creams, the leaves for lung and kidney irritations, the roots for digestive upsets. Marshmallow provides a mucus coating on the digestive system, so it's good for people with long-term digestive problems."

Could Nagata's be good for you?

"The marshmallow is in there and able to do its job," Stevens says. "It wouldn't be a therapeutic dose, but it would be soothing for the lining of the stomach. Definitely it would help rather than hurt."

When confectioners began making *pâte de guimauve*, as candy, not medicine, they used powdered marshmallow root, ground sugar, ground gum arabic, orange flower water, and egg whites. This didn't last. We assume that the marshmallow's story is one of 1950s food processing. In fact, by 1870, candy makers had already dropped the ingredient that gave marshmallows their name and reduced them to sugar, gelatin, egg whites, and flavouring.

In this form, the marshmallow became a popular homemade candy. My mother's copy of the United Farm Women of Alberta (UFWA) cookbook, first published in 1928, has three marshmallow recipes to choose from, and the B.C. government's dourly practical home economics textbook, *Foods and Home Management*, first printed in 1932, includes a chocolate marshmallow version, and the popular rolled-in-roasted-coconut variation.

Marshmallows you made at home were very similar to the ones the confectioner made at the candy store: small batches, poured into a tray, cut into squares and dredged with coconut, icing sugar, or arrowroot to seal their surfaces and keep them from drying out. Around 1920, everything changed. "Marshmallow manufacturers pooled their knowledge," a Kraft General Foods Canada Inc. handout explains, "and with the help of chemists, bacteriologists and home economists," they made "the better-looking, better-tasting and better-keeping marshmallow we know and love today."

In the 1920s, processing was nothing to criticize in a food, especially one that was white, pure, clean and untouched by human hands. It was at this point that marshmallows began to invade the dinner table. Laura Shapiro in *Perfection Salad*, a history of the home economics movement in North America, mentions a menu that combined baked beans and toasted marshmallows stuffed with raisins. Her analysis: the old-fashioned and economical baked bean was given new status by being garnished with marshmallows, "because sweets were very much a lady's way of assuaging her delicate hunger."

Shapiro's version of Perfection Salad is "cabbage, celery and red peppers, all chopped fine and bound by a plain aspic." The UFWA cookbook's Perfection Salad is chopped cabbage mixed with pineapple and marshmallow, with a whipped cream dressing. The more straightforward Marshmallow Salad calls for a pound of marshmallows, a small can of pineapples and a pound of white grapes. Contributor Mrs. P. Larson, from the UFWA's Nanton local, reports that it "will serve 20 people and will keep for days if kept in a cool place."

I would bet it could serve hundreds, but I might be wrong. Somebody must be making the 93 marshmallow recipes on the Kraft Interactive Kitchen's web site, including a "Classic" Waldorf salad—apples, mini-marshmallows, celery, walnuts, and Miracle Whip.

This recipe would not, by the way, be improved by substituting real marshmallows. Genuine or not, they remain sweet, squishy, and well outside the boundaries of serious food. "This is pretty much where it ends," Nagata says. "We're not going to drizzle aged balsamic on them, or tempura-fry them. Maybe we'll do some s'mores. But there is a line, and we're not crossing it."

Soda Water

IT'S UNSETTLING TO THINK OF YOURSELF AS A BUBBLE—A BRIEF, floating tumble through space, a pop and then oblivion. But if you are looking around at symbols for the brevity of human life, it's the one you'd best choose.

I found this out by accident. What I had intended to do was examine a small, nagging feeling I had of somehow being hoodwinked by soda water.

I buy soda water every week, when I buy milk. I drink it by itself and mix it with fruit concentrates: white grape, black currant, a mango syrup from Egypt that I found in an Iranian supermarket. That's $200 a year for bubbled water when I could satisfy my thirst for free, straight from the tap. And what do I get for my money? To tell the truth, I didn't really know.

Every once in a while, I'd put my hand around a cold can of soda water and get catapulted back to East 22nd Avenue in Vancouver, circa 1955. My father, standing at the kitchen sink, holding up a glass of water, would pose one of his favourite questions: "If you had the choice of just one thing to drink for the rest of your life, what would a smart person pick?" The only answer he accepted was water. It did me no good to argue that I didn't have to choose just one lifetime beverage, and for the moment I'd rather have something bubbly.

Plain water costs nothing in a restaurant. For soda water, you can easily pay $3. And what you get is a non-drink: no alcohol, no sugar, no caffeine. You get water with a pinch of sodium bicarbonate.

Nutritionists advise us to avoid sodium in all forms, and here I was putting out good money to ingest it. I was beginning to feel like the sort of affable gull the eighteenth century called a bubble. The *Oxford English Dictionary* also lists bubble as a transitive verb, meaning to befool, cheat, or humbug, as in: "he is to be bubbled of his mistress as of his money."

What was this bubble getting for her money? A crisp sensation across the roof of the mouth and over the tongue, the burning feeling of a thousand bubbles popping. For some reason, this fizz translated into a little rush of well-being, a lift. It's somehow festive, fun. Why should that be so? And what makes it worth paying for?

The first people who tried to put salted bubbles in water thought that the endeavour had medical importance. They were trying to duplicate healing natural springs, some of which bubbled. People had been travelling to such springs since at least 1300; how much better, for those who couldn't make the trip, if they could drink the same waters in a bottle at home.

Scottish chemist and physicist Joseph Black was the first to identify carbon dioxide as the gas inside the bubbles, in 1756. He called it "fixed air." In 1772, British clergyman and amateur chemist Joseph Priestley, better known for his discovery of oxygen, collected carbon dioxide gas from a nearby brewery—one of its many sources is fermenting beer—and bubbled the gas through water. He got what he called "an exceedingly pleasant sparkling water, resembling Seltzer water." (To Priestley, Seltzer water was a sparkling mineral water from the village of Nieder-Selters in Prussia.)

Priestley published his treatise, *Directions for Impregnating Water with Fixed Air, In order to communicate to it the peculiar Spirit and Virtues of Pyrmont Water, And other Mineral Waters of a similar*

EATING MY WORDS

Nature. He was awarded the Copley Medal from the Royal Society of London, particularly for his demonstration that some of the fixed air could be absorbed into the human bloodstream, where it combines with mild acids, giving relief to pains caused by over-acidic stomachs.

The original bottled health drink is now falling out of favour, for health reasons. In 1985, soda water held 60 per cent of the carbonated water market, with seltzer (carbonated water without the sodium bicarbonate) taking the other 40 per cent. Last year seltzer took 62 per cent of the market, and soda water 38 per cent. "People are just veering away from sodium where they can," said Helen Berry at the Beverage Marketing Association in New York.

How much sodium is there in soda water? Not enough for me to worry about. In Schweppes, it's 17.9 milligrams per 100 millilitres. The recommended daily allowance for sodium varies from 1,100 to 3,300 milligrams, depending on which expert you ask. One serving of canned soup can contain 1,000 to 1,500 milligrams of sodium. I swore off canned soup some time ago and am therefore prepared to face the consequences of 179 milligrams of sodium in a litre of sparkling water.

Still, I can't help thinking how surprised Priestley would be to see what his treatise has spawned. Soda water is the basis of a giant industry that sells three products: bubbles in water, sweet bubbles in water, and salted bubbles in water. Sweet bubbles in water is by far the most successful of the three products: in 1990, Americans consumed about two hundred litres of soft drinks per capita— about four litres a week for every man, woman, and child.

The soft drink industry sells its products through frenetically active advertising campaigns. The product it sells is fun. True, it's not quite the same grade of fun as champagne bubbles tickling your nose, but it's fun all the same. The advertising works, I think, because at some level we know that human beings don't live long. Bubbles are the only symbol of the brevity of life that makes the point in an agreeable way.

Take time to watch leaves fall, or walk for a while under

cherry trees late in spring, and you feel a perfectly understandable tug on the heart. Dead things fall down, or in the case of cherry blossoms, drift down.

Or trace the paths of sparks in the fireplace: they blaze and die into black. The truth of impermanence speaks out plainly from the fire, with Job's unhappy observation that "man is born to trouble as the sparks fly upward" echoing in the background.

Bubbles have just as good a claim to being symbols of the brevity of life. Here's a sampling of relevant quotations:

- "The world's a bubble and the life of man less than a span." – Francis Bacon
- "Like the dew on the mountain, like the foam on the river, like the bubble on the fountain, Thou art gone, and forever!" – Sir Walter Scott
- "Life's troubled bubble broken." – Walter de la Mare
- "And fear not lest Existence closing your Account and mine, should know the like no more. The Eternal Saki from that Bowl has pour'd millions of Bubbles like us, and will pour." – Edward Fitzgerald

But a fresh bottle of soda water is a different thing. When you open it, uncounted throngs of captive carbon dioxide molecules race up through the water to burst free at the surface. No wonder people in soft drink commercials—the quintessential happy bubbles—move at such a frantic pace. It's impossible not to smile at the sight of them, not to be charmed by the eagerness of their travels. We may be only bubbles too, but things that rush upward are alive.

Fast Food

HAVE YOU BEEN FEELING HURRIED LATELY? PRESSED? STRESSED? Moved along at a pace just a little faster than is entirely comfortable? Then I've got news for you. Your sense of hurry could be connected to fast food. I am not talking here about golden arches or Wendy's or Burger King. Don't bother telling me that you haven't had a franchise hamburger in years. It doesn't matter. All of our food is fast food.

This is not a question of how we cook, although logic says that our frantic rush to cook meals faster and faster contributes its own small sense of desperation about time. Not too long ago a cookbook that promised a meal in an hour was thought to be speedy. Now thirty minutes is the outside limit for cookbooks that claim to speed. Marian Burros, food columnist for *The New York Times*, has published an entire book of twenty-minute menus. We can only assume that, like the four-minute mile, the ten-minute meal will be tackled and the battle won.

But that is not what I am talking about. Our food is literally fast.

No matter how slowly you cook a chicken, that chicken is fast food, because it grew from chick to three-pound broiler in six weeks. In 1950, the same weight gain took twelve weeks. What difference does it make? On the surface, none. But then, we aren't talking about surfaces. A yoga teacher once told me that a certain pose was best understood "on a molecular level." It's not a level I often find myself on. But I suspect that for thinking about fast food, molecular is the way to go.

Chickens are prime examples of the increased velocity of modern food. But hurried-up chickens are by no means an isolated case. In the 1940s, it took an average pig seven to eight months to put on enough weight to go to market. In 1991 the gain takes 5 $\frac{1}{2}$ to 6 months. Pick up any issue of the *Western Hog Journal*, the quarterly magazine of the pork production industry, and you will hear the ever-quickening beat: more, faster. The advertisers say it best. Posistac, a brand of the antibiotic salinomycin, "moves 'em out faster." The accompanying photograph shows the back ends of healthy hogs headed up a ramp—which we might reasonably expect to be high on a list of a pig farmer's favourite views of pigs. Tylan growth-promoting feed additives promise "fewer days to market." Akzo's P.G. 600, an estrus-inducing hormone, assures "earlier breeding," among other benefits, and Stafac, an antibiotic that reduces bacteria in the pig's gut, will help them "gain weight faster and get to market sooner."

Beginning around the Second World War, poultry farmers began to breed specialist hens—layers and broilers. The layers were bred for egg production, the broilers for the speed with which they could put on weight. Pigs too were bred for their growth rate, which is 25 to 30 per cent inheritable. The next step was scientific feeding. No more slops for pigs, but a mix of twenty or thirty ingredients tailored to the animals' needs.

It isn't just animal food that is moving at a quicker pace. In fact, there is a sense in which we have been speeding up the life of the plant foods we eat ever since we first embarked on farming. For ten thousand years farmers have been selecting the hardiest, the quickest to produce, the sweetest, the most productive among the plants. What's changed is that lately we've become breathtakingly good at it.

Take, for example, Wisconsin Fast Plants, the invention of Paul Williams, Professor of Plant Pathology at the University of

Wisconsin in Madison. Williams, who was born in Vancouver and studied plant science at the University of B.C., took a small, wild relative of the turnip, found in its native state on hillsides in Nepal, and used it to create a new plant—one that can move from seed to seed ten times in a year. That's ten times faster than many of the plants in our gardens, and five times faster than the *Brassica rapa* that Williams started with. He selected the parent plant to work with because it was the quickest to flower of the two thousand brassicas in the U.S. Department of Agriculture's National Plant Germ Plasm System. Williams crossed quick-flowering plants with quick-flowering plants and raised them in his office so they would be, he says, "human-habitat friendly." His office is, admittedly, hot and bright—24°C (75°F), continuously illuminated with high-intensity light from cool white fluorescent lamps. "I've got a little population in front of me that's flowering in eleven days," he said over the phone from Wisconsin. "That's plenty fast."

Is there a limit to how fast plants can grow?

"There has to be a limit somewhere," Williams says. "But we keep pushing the limit genetically, and it keeps receding." Wisconsin Fast Plants now grow in fifty-five countries, and are being used by approximately two thousand scientists. They're used in classrooms—living organisms that can act out genetic theory before students' eyes.

Researchers are now breeding a faster-maturing canola with genes from fast plants, so northern B.C., Alberta, and Saskatchewan can grow oil seeds. Chinese scientists are using them to produce a rapid-growing Chinese cabbage.

Not surprisingly, a group is also working to isolate the gene that determines the ability to grow fast—or, more likely, Williams says, "a group of genes, working in concert." None of this is news to anyone who keeps track of agribusiness. Intensive speeding up of food production has been going on for the past fifty years, and shows no signs of stopping.

After all, why should it? More and faster food production is better, isn't it? In any case, we certainly don't want to go hungry while we thrash out the next big conundrum: Is growing more food faster the same kind of solution as building more freeways to move cars faster? Is the net effect the same—more people and more cars?

Meanwhile, what about the connection between fast food and ever more hurried lives?

Most of us accept the idea that we are what we eat. What we don't have is a good definition of food. Here is my best shot at a definition: food is that part of the life chain that we have declared to be edible. All food either is alive or was alive. We sustain ourselves by eating the residue of other lives.

It's possible to be unconscious of the lives we eat, but we can't disconnect ourselves from them, any more than a fish can separate itself from water.

So if the life that we take into our bodies at the dinner table is cycling faster and faster from birth to death, might we not begin to feel a certain internal sense of being rushed?

If we could feel it on a molecular level, I suspect it would feel hurried.

Bedevilled Eggs

IT'S TAKING LONGER TO DO THE GROCERY SHOPPING THESE DAYS. I lose time at the egg case, telling myself that eggs are the least expensive form of animal protein in the grocery store, that eggs make omelettes and frittatas, that eggs must be on hand if you want to make lemon meringue pie. But as I reach my hand out for a carton of Grade A large, I can't help seeing the hen that came first. Egg cartons, row upon row, somehow bring to mind the rows on rows of hens that produced them, layered in cages in battery houses.

My grandmother got all of her eggs by reaching into a nest. My mother did the same until she left the farm. I reach into a supermarket display case, trading a dark henhouse and clucking hens for bright lights and muzak. I save time, but the eggs I eat are bedevilled eggs. Try as poultry farmers do to persuade me that the hen in her cage is sitting pretty—warm, dry, and safe from terrors in the night—I can't buy it. A life passed in a small wire cage offends me, even if it no longer offends the chickens.

Poultry breeders have been working on the White Leghorn's personality, and if we are to believe reports, North America's premiere laying hen is now so passive that she doesn't want to scratch in a barnyard, so bred away from broodiness that the thought of chicks never forms in her brain. She is, if we are to take the no-

nonsense stance of industrial egg producers, a machine that breathes. But here we run smack into a universal law, as applicable to mathematics as it is to marriage: you don't change one side of an equation without changing the other. Turning hens into machines doesn't just provide us with inexpensive eggs. It cheapens our idea of hens and drains away their meaning as creatures who draw breath, like ourselves.

I won't deny that I have a special regard for chickens, forged when I played the role of the Little Red Hen in the Grade 1 class play. In *The Chicken Book*, Page Smith and Charles Daniel call this poultry heroine "the Protestant hen," so wholeheartedly does she live the work ethic. The Little Red Hen, frugal and hard-working, decides to make a loaf of bread to feed her chicks, and asks each one of her barnyard neighbours for help. The rat, the dog, and the pig—some versions use other animals in the supporting roles—all refuse in turn. "Then I will do it myself," says the Little Red Hen, and plants grain, threshes it, mills it, and bakes it into bread. When the bread is baked, she first asks which animals will help her eat it, and then gleefully refuses them—those who don't work, don't eat, after all—and feeds it to her chicks. She may be a bit of a Margaret Thatcher, but who can blame her?

The Protestant hen was particularly beloved by the Victorians. Not only did she work hard and produce, but in her barnyard family life, she reflected back to them the perfect working of the family unit. Smith and Daniel tell us that "the splendor of the cock and the simple comeliness of the hen comported almost ideally with the Victorian male's image of himself in relation to the opposite sex, and there is no doubt that the popularity of 'domestic fowl' with upper-class Victorians was in part a consequence of the relative ease with which they could be transformed into symbols of domestic felicity in human society."

Long before the Victorians, people valued roosters for their fighting spirit, and one theory holds that it was cockfighting, and not eggs, that prompted domestication. Chicks are renowned for flightiness, which may be why we are "chicken" when we're frightened. We can be "as mad as a wet hen," even though people who raise poultry say that wet hens aren't especially grumpy. Mostly we interpret the character of the barnyard hen as contented, lively, and industrious, and not too long on brains. At moments when the answer to lack of time appears to be doing more things faster, it's instructive to know that there's such a thing as being "as busy as a chicken scratching a hole in a tin plate."

In the four thousand years that *Gallus gallus*, descendant of an Indian jungle fowl, has been living with people, the hen's most hallowed role was to show us a model of protective motherhood. The normally flighty hen turns into a tiger when she has chicks. In the face of danger she puffs up her feathers and stands her ground; the chicks run underneath and shelter there. In the Bible, the mother hen mirrors the protective love of God. The psalmist sings—with the standard Judeo-Christian confusion over the sex of both God and mother hen—"he will cover you with his pinions, and under his wings you will find refuge." The god who chose to be a man knew the sex of hens. If we can credit the reports, He said: "Oh Jerusalem, Jerusalem, killing the prophets and stoning those who are sent to you! How often would I have gathered your children together as a hen gathers her brood under her wings, and you would not."

Farmers have always frustrated the hen's desire to see chicks come from her eggs, exploiting her characteristic behaviour of accumulating a clutch of eggs before she sits. Hens are not good at counting, so as long as one "nest egg" is left in place, most hens will contentedly lay for long periods, without becoming broody. But something eventually clicks, and hens begin to hide their eggs, acting innocent until they have their clutch, and then sitting. Thwarting broody hens was a constant battle on the part of small-scale chicken keepers. The pre-modern response to a determinedly broody hen was to let her have her way: find the nest, move it into the henhouse, and let her sit.

Modern agribusiness hens outlay their old-fashioned sisters two and three times over, cackling out close to an egg a day for the less than two years of their productive lives. They never waste time hatching eggs. As is usually the case with agribusiness productivity, there are downsides. Hens are no longer part of the kitchen economy, eating table scraps, bugs, and a little grain, and recycling their droppings into the vegetable garden. A little chicken manure can be the magic ingredient in the vegetable plot. Assembled in vast quantities, it's a pollutant. In concentrating animals and their wastes, we have taken a solution and neatly separated it into two problems, as Wendell Berry notes in his book of essays, *The Unsettling of America: Culture & Agriculture.*

Until the twentieth century, nobody made a lot of money selling eggs. For one thing, hens took the winters off. They stopped laying eggs in late fall and picked up again in the spring. For the cook, that meant eggs were expensive and old in winter, if you could find them at all. For the would-be large-scale egg producer, it meant four months of feeding birds that would not lay.

As early as the 1880s, farmers had begun to use incubators, relieving the hen of the necessity of bringing off her eggs. By 1930, poultry farmers knew that hens could be persuaded to lay all winter if they had enough light. From those two discoveries followed all the rest: the battery house, the wire cage, the flock of 100,000 birds, the clipped beak so hens living in close quarters will not peck each other to death for lack of something better to do.

Back in the days of small-scale poultry rearing, male chicks were raised until they weighed three pounds, then sold as "spring chickens." But young White Leghorn roosters don't put on flesh like a chicken bred for broiling. Nature, always slow on the uptake, is still producing roughly 50 per cent roosters, most of which are then burned or fed to pigs as soon as they can be sexed.

The egg I reach for in the supermarket rolls toward me down the gently sloping floor of a battery cage onto a conveyor belt and along the belt into a packing room. I never touch a hen when I reach for an egg, but she touches me.

Samuel Butler once said that a hen is just an egg's way of making another egg. In the last century, we've taken firmer control of the situation. Forget the eggs: a hen is just a poultry producer's way of turning feed into money.

Our world is very cold and mechanical sometimes. Whose wings will shelter us now?

Round Food
with a Hole in the Middle

THERE IS A REASON PEOPLE BELIEVE IN THE RESURRECTED ELVIS, buy pantyhose in egg-shaped packages, and eat chicken rings. It's this: we can't help seeing and responding to symbols, even when we don't know what they mean. Let us loose in the vicinity of a potent form we don't consciously understand and there's no telling what we'll do.

Chicken rings, for those who haven't seen them on a fast-food menu or stumbled across them in the supermarket's poultry freezer, are breaded, deep-fried circles, usually formed from ground-up chicken—a circular nugget if you like.

I doubt that the inventor of chicken rings studied the ruins of the five hundred stone circles that dot Great Britain, or stared at a Tibetan mandala, or at the round rose window at Notre Dame, and said: "Eureka, this is the way to sell more chicken!" There was no need to, because the happiness value of what we might as well call "round food with a hole in the middle" is well known. When Lois Arnold, speaking for Québec's Maxi Poultry, told me the chicken ring her company launched was doing well with children "because of the fun," we both knew what she meant.

Small fingers can wear onion rings and doughnut rings. Small, unsupervised fingers can twirl them until they fly off the end and land—well, who cares where they land? Baby fingers spend happy moments picking Cheerios up off the high-chair tray. The best way to eat a LifeSaver candy—although this takes the skills of at least an eight-year-old—is to suck it until the ring is so thin you can stick your little finger through the hole.

Round foods with a hole in the middle are a branch of the larger, equally well-liked family of round and spherical foods. Only a chronic dyspeptic can suppress a little rush of affection toward pizza, cookies, hamburgers, cakes, cupcakes, muffins, pies, pancakes, barbecued pork buns, and the whole world of spherical fruits. They all say "playtime" in one way or another, simply by virtue of their shape. Eat a round food and you are eating not just food but symbol, and a satisfying symbol at that: unity, wholeness, the infinitely big and infinitely small zero.

Think of potters' wheels, chariot wheels, the earth, the sun, the moon. It's no wonder that the circle is a sacred form. From Egypt to Tibet, the mandala, a circle divided into segments, has stood as a symbol for the whole self for thousands of years. Zen masters in Japan draw perfect freehand circles in brush and ink as a sign of their enlightenment; our own tradition has thirteenth-century Florentine painter Giotto astonishing Pope Benedict and his art advisers with the same feat. Oglala Sioux medicine man Black Elk, the nineteenth century's most eloquent communicator of the native American world view, stated a basic fact of pre-modern cultures when he said: "The power of the world always works in circles and everything tries to be round."

When we turn from round food to round food with a hole in the middle, we find another layer of meaning. In *The Power of the Center: A Study of Composition in the Visual Arts*, Rudolf Arnheim writes that human beings live in two spatial systems: grids and concentric circles. The grid system exists because when we stand on the earth, it's flat beneath our feet. Grids give us right angles, ups and downs, ways to map physical reality. What a grid lacks is a centre. Arnheim calls spatial organization by concentric circles the "cosmic" system. It's the natural arrangement for solar systems and atoms. What it offers is a hierarchy: importance is determined by closeness to the centre of the circle. This centre is T.S. Eliot's "still point of the turning world." It's the spot in the middle, where all the movement at the outside edge of the wheel translates into a quiet hum of pure energy. It's where the mystics tell us our hearts live.

Not all concentric circles are positive. The bull's eye in a target and the sucking centre of a whirlpool are circles on the dark side of human life. Circles in the realm of light hold a deep sense of safety at their centres; we yearn to be there. Maybe it's just a happy accident that we rescue people from drowning by throwing them a cork ring—a lifesaver. Psychic rescue is generally judged complete when the flailing person finds a centre.

As overwrought as this may sound, I think a chicken ring is a circle of the dark side. They were spawned in the 1980s, another attempt to wring more variety from breaded, ground-up chicken, along with nuggets, fingers, and patties. They have never taken a huge bite out of the "further processing" chicken market, but they've never entirely gone away. A web search suggests that chicken rings have found a niche market in school cafeterias, popping up regularly on the menus for web-savvy schools located in places like Glencoe, Oklahoma, and Greenville, Texas. The Southern Baptist Educational Center, located a little southeast of Memphis, served them five times in one month, accompanied, on one occasion, with creamed potatoes and gravy, buttered corn, and corn bread.

The usual way to make them is this: 1,000 kilograms (2,200 pounds) of chicken meat is loaded into a mixing machine and ground until it takes on the texture of mayonnaise. To form the ring, an arm reaches out over the goo, an arm with doughnut-shaped rings lining its bottom edge. Vacuum power sucks the chicken mush up into the rings. The arm swings out over a tray coated with seasoned bread crumbs. A poking thing knocks the rings down into the breading mixture, and the tray carries them away to be partially fried, frozen, and packaged. Maxi Poultry's marketing vice-president Terry Irwin says that its chicken rings are not cut, mixed, or ground. Instead, Maxi presses chicken breasts to a uniform thickness, a sort of flowing blanket of chicken flesh, and then cuts rings.

In either case, you have what is ostensibly a round food with a hole in the middle. But if you fix your attention on the still centre of a chicken ring, these thoughts might occur to you. Onions already come in rings. Squid can easily be cut into rings. LifeSavers start as syrup, and doughnuts and Cheerios start life as shapeless batters. The ingredients of a batch of chicken rings once had enough coherence to walk around clucking.

It seems shocking, somehow sacreligious. Human beings already experience what Leon Kass, in *The Hungry Soul*, calls the great paradox of eating: "That to preserve their life and form, living forms necessarily destroy life and form." Even when there's no meat on the table, the destruction continues. Much of what we eat is seeds: corn, wheat, rice, lentils, beans—each one a potential life, each life extinguished, ground into a slurry and assimilated.

Do we really have to do it twice?

The Fat of the Land
Is Passé

I WAS STANDING AT THE DAIRY CASE, DECIDING WHICH KIND OF yogurt to buy, when I suddenly felt a little blue chill—a chill the exact colour of skim milk in a white bowl. I buy plain yogurt. My choice had to do with how much fat I wanted—3.5 per cent, 2 per cent, or 0.5 per cent butterfat. I only had two dollars with me, which, it turned out, was enough to buy a tub of whole-milk yogurt. But in that store at least, I was nineteen cents short of yogurt with reduced fat. I raised my eyes and took in the rows of 1-per cent milk cartons, mountains of part-skim mozzarella, and stacked tubs of "lite" cream cheese.

That's when the chill arrived. At that moment I realized that butterfat, the cow's crowning glory and the measure of her milk's worth, is slipping out of the dairy case. Fat does generally slip, slide, lubricate. You can expect a pat of butter to roll down an ear of corn, slide off a stack of pancakes, sink into the holes in a crumpet. But this is different. Let's take 1-per cent milk as an example. Introduced in 1989, it has almost overtaken skim milk in sales and shows no signs of levelling off. I buy it. Like most other 1-per cent drinkers, I used to buy 2-per cent milk. Millions of people, all over the continent, are making the same choice.

So where does the leftover butterfat go? Is there, somewhere just outside of Ottawa, a national butter stockpile? And if we no longer want butterfat in our milk, how does that affect the cultural status of butter?

As so often happens, the answer to these questions is best reached by means of a detour, this time into the strange and increasingly unfamiliar world of milk. When she was very small, my sister was of the firm belief that milk grows in bottles. We are, by and large, not much better informed. Milk grows in factories now, but the farmer still gets it from a cow, albeit a much larger animal than before, with three times the yearly milk production of her pre-industrial ancestors. The cow must still give birth to a calf before the milk will flow.

Human beings are the only animal that routinely drinks cow's milk, or as militant vegetarians would have it, the nursing secretions of a major mammal.

Very few human beings in the world continue to drink milk after childhood. Most adults stop being able to digest a milk sugar called lactose. If they eat dairy products at all, they eat lactose-free forms, such as yogurt and butter. As far as pouring a cool glass of moo juice goes, it's pretty much us, the Northern Europeans, and the Masai.

Whether people drink it or eat it as yogurt and butter, milk is a highly charged food, a sacred substance. Milk means wealth and plenty; milk and honey flow in the land we long to find. There are two reasons why milk is holy. First, it is an animal food that comes to us untainted by the blood of the animal—only eggs and honey share this innocent purity. Cows give more milk than calves need. A calf is soon weaned; a cow will give milk for ten months after giving birth. Furthermore, this pure white liquid can be transformed into solid food: cream, butter, yogurt, and cheese. Cream is milk taken to a higher level. Mixed in the milk as it comes from the cow, it rises to the top as the milk sits.

Our word cream comes from a Greek word, *chrism*, which means oil for anointing. The Romans borrowed the word from the Greeks; they both understood it to mean olive oil. The northern barbarians borrowed "chrism" from the Romans and applied it to the one food they had that was equally rich and runny. "Chrism" is also the root of the word Christ—the anointed one, the cream, so to speak, of the crop.

In butter, milk reaches its highest form: golden, richer even than cream, solid, but capable of melting back into a liquid state. Butter is achieved by churning cream until the fat globules join together and float out of the milk. Churning is itself magical. Pounding, twisting paddles beat solid butter out of liquid cream. Churning is a symbol of creativity; when we churn things around in our minds, we expect an idea to solidify like a lump of butter in milk.

Farmers have traditionally been paid, and cows prized, for the butterfat content of their milk. My mother's family kept a Jersey cow, called Buttercup, whose rich milk was always reserved for the baby of the year. Butterfat was good, a benign substance often used as a medicine. In her exhaustive chapter on butter in *Much Depends on Dinner*, Margaret Visser tells us that the Celtic word for butter means ointment. And the sixteenth century had a "strange but widely used" remedy for pain in the joints: butter, left to liquefy several days in the sun, and then drunk.

Now we are afraid that butterfat will kill us. Cream is an artery clogger; butter greases the skids to the grave. But while few actually want to give up eating cheese or ice cream, you will not find many people who think life isn't worth living without whole milk. When millions of people decide to cut butterfat in their milk, the decision—or more correctly, the millions of decisions—change the dairy business.

Modern dairying is divided into two major categories: fluid milk and industrial milk. You buy fluid milk in a carton or bottle, and industrial milk in butter and cheese. When innumerable hands reach out, again and again, for one-per cent milk, the fluid-milk processing plant comes up with a surplus of butterfat. Large dairies use the excess butterfat to make ice cream, butter, and cheese. Smaller dairies are more likely to sell it outside, to a specialized butter-and-cheese maker.

So far, so good. But dairies that used to depend on industrial milk for their butterfat now have a more concentrated supply from the fluid market. They don't need to buy as much whole milk. Farmers who produce for the butter and cheese industries are losing their customers.

In the past, when we drank our butterfat in our milk, Canada had a giant skim milk surplus incurred on the way to making butter. Some was sold for animal feed. The Canadian Dairy Commission bought what was left over—148 million kilograms in 1975–'76. By 1989–'90, the dairy commission's purchases had tumbled to 56 million kilograms. They are still falling, to an estimated 48 million kilograms in 1990–'91. Nelson Coyle, policy analyst for the dairy commission, says: "We have roughly 15 per cent of our production to thin out. It's quite a blow to producers." In 1940, Canadians slathered 10.81 kilograms of butter per capita over our bread. In 1989, per capita consumption was 3.61 kilograms. We may still try to butter people up, but we can hardly lay it on as thick as we used to.

Meanwhile, milk has lost some of its innocent appeal, at least to those who see it as the socially acceptable side of the veal-calf industry. A glass of milk, after all, can't be had without a calf coming first. Male calves, like male laying chicks, are redundant in an industry that needs only a few sires to impregnate the herd—by proxy, of course. Most male dairy calves spend a brief, anemic life in containment before they are slaughtered for "white" veal.

We may still know what side our bread is buttered on, and expect the cream to take its rightful place at the top of the milk bottle, but when it does, we remove it as a danger to health. Perhaps it won't be long before we start talking in admiring tones about people who live off the skim of the land.

Culinary Roots

CULINARY ROOTS COME IN ALL SHAPES AND SIZES: CARROTS, radishes, memories, recipes. The universal truth of culinary roots is this: if the roots are strong and healthy, then so is the fruit.

Want an example of culinary rootedness? Take a look at *Italy, a Culinary Journey*, with its lavish photographs of Italy's culinary regions. Liguria, Lazio, Toscana, Umbria, Abruzzo, Sicilia, Lombardia, Sardinia: each one defined by its characteristic wine, its oil, its fruits and vegetables. In each case, the cooking developed from the food of the region. People ate what was available, and if you were in a different place, you ate different food. Even within regions there are differences. "As you travel eastwards in Liguria, leaving Provençe behind, you will begin to taste the difference at the table," writes Vilma Pesciallo Garabaghi, one of the book's fourteen contributing writers. "The pesto will have become a little lighter in flavour and colour. You will find it served on trenette, a local variety of ribbon pasta."

When we turn to the food of our own region, pickings are thinner. The Pacific Coast has had 120 years of European settlement. So far, our most substantial contribution to world cuisine is the Nanaimo Bar. While a Nanaimo Bar is a fine thing in its own way, if this is the fruit it does make you question the state of our roots.

What can I tell you after digging about in our culinary roots?

The quick answer is that we don't have them. This is unfortunate, because culinary roots perform the same services for regional cuisines that physical roots do for plants and psychological roots do for people. Roots hold us steady, plants and humans alike, and more important still, they feed us. In plants, what actually does the eating is the root hair, or rather hairs—as many as two hundred on a square centimetre of root tissue. How sensitive are they? How deeply can they penetrate?

Roots have skin, as we do. What happens is that one of the epidermal cells sends out an extension, a root hair one cell thick. The filament grows out in search of water and food. It lives in the soil for a few days or a few weeks in what we can only imagine as the most intimate contact. Every area has a distinct soil, its qualities determined by which and how much of the following variables are present: air, water, mineral particles, soluble chemical compounds, organic matter, and living organisms. Each soil breathes a different message to the root hair; the root hair sends its message along to the plant. When we get the message, we call it taste. It can be very distinct, and very desirable, which is why the French bother to make official demarcations of the vineyards that can lay claim to the special taste of the soil.

This is what makes us inhabitants of the twentieth century so unusual. We are the first people in history to conduct a massive experiment in not eating the food that grows where we do. What made great cuisines develop was not just good food but isolation. Ligurian cooks might have reached gladly for black truffles, but the truffles weren't there to reach for. Tuscans didn't drink Chianti out of sentiment or regional loyalty. They drank it because that's what they grew, and they raised the cooking of what they grew into an art. We, on the other hand, have conquered transportation. Refrigerator trucks hurtle north to B.C. up the road from California, freighters plow across the ocean from New Zealand, air freight zooms in from Taiwan. The Central Intelligence Agency, concerned about the vulnerability of the U.S. food system, did a study to find the average distance food travels from the farm to the table. The answer: 2200 kilometres (1,365 miles). We may look at the supermarket and think we see a food warehouse. What we're really seeing is the last ripple in a river of food.

With modern transportation we have succeeded in obliterating not just regions but seasons. If you hold a radish in your hands, you are holding a certain kind of culinary root. If you are holding a radish in Vancouver in January, then you are holding culinary rootlessness—the food of any time, any place, not the food of here, now.

It is possible to trace the out-of-season radish, of course. If it has the tops on, it probably came from California. If it's in a cellophane bag with the greens trimmed off, then it probably came from Florida, perhaps from the farm of Duda & Sons, where they plant forty acres of radishes a day, every day for nine months of the year.

I don't want to return to winters without fresh fruit. In fact, it's hard not to be fond of an economic system that brings mangoes in April. I'd be ready to believe that our food system is an unlimited boon if it weren't for two things.

The first is that it's hard to buy local produce even when it's in season. Unless you shop the produce markets and drive to farmers' stands, you can go a whole summer without seeing local strawberries. Supermarket chains don't work on the scale of local berry farmers; they work on the scale of Duda & Sons. In *The Taste of America*, their book on the desperate state of North American food, John and Karen Hess have this plaintive statement on the tomato. "In the old Washington Market, in tomato time, one could find ripe fruit, tart, sweet and bursting with juice. Now, there is not a ripe-picked tomato to be found even in tomato time. So we can have tomatoes year-round, but now we cannot buy tomatoes worth eating at any time of year."

Something very strange has happened—a reversal of the conditions that applied for all the generations of cooks who preceded us. Sometime after the Second World War, we crossed the line. Today, if you had a choice of vows to make—the first, that you would not eat anything grown further than 800 kilometres (500 miles) from where you live, and the second, that you would not eat anything grown closer than 800 kilometres to where you live—it would be much, much easier and probably less expensive, to choose to eat outside the 800-kilometre limit, especially in winter.

What a madcap touch that is. You can almost see the carnival display in some future circus of environmental horrors: step right up, folks, and see the people who convinced themselves that profitable food is the same as economical food, that imported food, no matter what the cost might be in fossil fuels, is somehow less expensive than food grown in the region.

Meanwhile, land that could feed us is being lost to development. Working farms near a city are always worth much less than the same land, subdivided and turned into condos and strip malls—as long as we can get lots of cheap food from other places, and as long as we don't particularly care about our culinary roots.

But there it is: the root and the fruit so intimately joined. After all, just because we don't have culinary roots doesn't mean we don't have a regional cuisine. The region, the economic whole that delivers food to our stores, is North America. And the regional cuisine?

Ask yourself: What is the food of the poor, the food you have to make efforts to get away from, the food that is offered at every turn, the food that is always available? Yes, our regional cuisine is fast food—hamburgers, fries, fried chicken, chips, milkshakes, and pizza. Our *vin du pays* is pop. Move up the scale just a little and it's Buffalo chicken wings, Cajun chicken strips, iceberg lettuce, surf and turf plates, and radishes in plastic bags.

You want to change the fruit? Change the root.

Famine

NEWS OF FAMINE IS NEVER WELCOME. I RUN AWAY FROM IT, myself. Once the wizened babies start showing up on the screen nightly at 10 p.m., I'm gone. I might tune in long enough to find out if the old patterns are once more in place—starving villagers, bumbling bureaucrats, greedy politicians, rapacious generals—but then I get out while I've got a hope of maintaining tranquility.

I think my fellow cowards are legion. Who can bear the news of starvation? Make no mistake about what's happening. We see dying children on the news not just because they feed the television camera the strongest images. They do, of course, but they are also the ones who starve to death.

In a famine, the strongest eat first: men, then women, then children and old people. Children vastly outnumber old people in the developing world. In a famine, large numbers of children die.

Letting our children starve, as a human behaviour, defies explanation. We don't, after all, have a worldwide food shortage. It's just that the poorest people can't afford to buy it.

We have communication and transportation systems that are unparalleled in world history—we can bounce pictures by satellite from the Middle East to Washington D.C. in two seconds. Yet in 1991, more than six months passed after satellites told us that the crops had failed in the Sudan and that disaster awaited. Two seconds, by the way, is becoming infamous as the normal interval between child deaths from poverty on this sad earth of ours. Even when there is no crisis on the Iraqi border, no famine in the Sudan, or Somalia, no cyclone in Bangladesh, 15 million children die each year of hunger-related causes. These little rivulets of death at random intervals—whooping cough in one village, measles in another—average out to one every two seconds.

All a famine does is make the starving news, and bring the face of hunger into our living rooms. I am tired of looking at it, sick of the guilt of living in a well-fed part of the world. So I would like to suggest that we try to think about hunger in a different way for a while. I know the model I'm about to use is inadequate. I don't have an analogy for world hunger that doesn't break sooner or later under the weight. So I've done the best I can with what I have. I hope you'll excuse me.

Here is what I think: The wealthy nations of the world are now in the position of the man or woman who has begun to realize that every romantic prospect has the same fatal flaw. Each one—feel free to choose your favourite defect—is jealous and clinging, or a flirt and philanderer, or walks in the great army of the intimacy-impaired. After a certain number of catastrophes, only the most opaque could fail to ask if the problem is not really our own. Suspicion grows that the fault lies in the selecting mechanism.

This principle has broad possibilities of application. Being in one car accident, for example, is bad luck. Being in three car accidents bears study. One famine might be attributed to crop failure. One experience of watching starving babies on our televisions might lead us to imagine that there is something intractable in that particular situation, some reason that explains death by hunger in the twentieth century. But Bangladesh, Ethiopia, the Sudan? Each succeeds the other in turn; each one comes back for replays every few years. Famine is not some accident that strikes at humanity from nowhere. The problem is not ignorant peasant farmers or malevolent weather. Famine is part of the way the world economy works. Hunger for the poorest is as much a part of the world economy as caviar is for the most wealthy.

To claim the problem as our own does not have many immediate benefits, personal or global. At first it seems to make the problem worse, for it takes away our hope that a lover who is just right is out there somewhere, that a self-sufficient Third World might some day just sort of pop up on the evening news. But after a while, things improve. Watch long enough and you will see the place where the troublesome behaviour begins. At first you can't do anything much about it except be aware, but it's a psychological maxim that any of your own behaviours you can observe, calmly and without blame, you can eventually control.

Where does hunger begin? Global indebtedness is one. To get cash to service the debt, you need cash crops, so less land can be planted in staples. Some countries export staple crops to get foreign exchange. Famine experts believe the Sudan had been exporting grain, most of it to be used as animal feed. Low commodity prices are another root of hunger. What brings a high dollar on the international market is not coffee beans or cocoa, but computers and military equipment. The nations of what is now being called the Fourth World, the ones in which hunger is epidemic, are the nations that don't have anything we want to buy.

In theory we are committed to helping these nations become self-sufficient. Canada, like all other western nations, has pledged to give 0.7 per cent of gross national product to development. So far only the Scandinavian countries have lived up to the commitment. In 1991, Canada's budget allotted 0.47 per cent, but only when export development loans and aid to Eastern Europe—previously not part of the equation—were lumped in. In the 2001 to 2002 fiscal year, Canada gave 0.27 per cent of GNP to international development.

When I was a child, we had a record called "It's in the Book," a comedy routine based on the nursery rhyme Little Bo Peep. As you will recall, Little Bo Peep lost her sheep and didn't know where to find them. She is advised to leave them alone, and assured that they'll come home, dragging their tails behind them. The comedian works himself into apoplexy unravelling the absurdities of this rhyme. "If the sheep were lost, and she couldn't find them, then she'd *have* to leave them alone, wouldn't she?" he shrieks, voicing all the impotent futility of looking for what we lack.

It is baffling to sit with the images of dying babies. How can it be that these children are somehow in full view of television cameras and yet outside the reach of help? Again and again, they bring our attention back to the economic system that spawns famine, the political divisions that prevent distribution of aid. And there, in the gap between what we can see and what we can do, is the face of hunger.

WORDS FOR EATING,
FOOD FOR THOUGHT

Why I Quit My Job
as a Restaurant Critic

IN 1987, LIFE—CLEVERLY DISGUISED AS A COUPLE OF SENIOR editors at *The Vancouver Sun* —offered me a free lunch. All I had to do was write once a week about a restaurant, preferably modest in price, and I could spend company money eating out. Naturally I bit.

After all, who hasn't wanted to be a restaurant critic? To read menus with a blithe disregard for the bill; to step out of the role of hapless paying customer, who has limited recourse if the meal falls far short of its promise; to become a sort of culinary Robin Hood, rewarding the good and chastising the indifferent—it has to be wonderful, right?

Well, sort of.

There is nothing more tedious than hearing someone in a privileged position whine. So I will tell you about my years as a restaurant critic with as little complaint as I can manage. It was privileged. I loved it, and I want to do it again someday fairly soon. But I wouldn't be telling the truth if I didn't write the dark side too.

It all began pleasantly enough. Shortly after I started writing restaurant reviews, I noticed that people at parties had more to say to me. Everyone has a restaurant recommendation—or wants one. Everyone has a story to tell about eating out. Everyone, it seems, wants to know what it's like to be a restaurant critic. My phone rang more often. In three years of writing about visual arts, I don't remember getting any requests for the name of a good gallery to take Mother to for an afternoon, or the right place for the visiting cousins from Toronto to see local art. But restaurants? My opinion was in demand.

It got busy. Editors for guidebooks began to call. Since I was compiling an informal guide to city restaurants week by week, just by doing my job, it made sense to take on more work. One winter, I wrote my weekly column and worked on two guidebooks at the same time. My husband, Alan, remembers this period as breakfast, lunch, and dinner out every day for six weeks. My memory is that it started slower: dinner out five nights the first week, five dinners and two lunches the next, a breakfast or two added into the third, and so on, until, at the end, I just carried the restaurant list with me and checked another one off at every meal.

I didn't get tired of eating out, even then.

Once you have ordered a dinner that promises to be splendid, once you are drinking a glass of wine, fingering the napkin, watching the candles flicker, making end-of-the-day conversation with someone you like very much, life is a wonderful dream. The problem for a restaurant critic is that this dream belongs to someone else—someone much wealthier.

Restaurant critics come in two main forms: celebrity and incognito. I chose to be incognito. There are advantages to both approaches. I know this because when I was in my mid-twenties I kept company for three years with a highly recognizable restaurant critic. I remember dinners in French restaurants; we sat at the best table in the house, the waiters were attentive, the owners beamed with joy as they brought us special little tidbits from the kitchen. Everyone was very glad to see us wherever we went, and the food was always as good as it could be. But I wanted to report on what any given restaurant was like for the average paying customer. And I knew from experience that the restaurant you visit with a well-known critic is not the same restaurant you visit with a girlfriend a week later.

My decision was also a question of temperament. I like privacy. And I frequently find myself without much to say, especially before I've been fed. If your face is known, you are condemned to clanging around in the restaurant critic's role, always on show. If it isn't, you can slip into a restaurant, have a meal and slip out again—and do the required interview with the owner or the chef over the phone.

I thought I had managed to evade the nastier parts of the role. So you can imagine my dismay when I woke up to find myself trapped inside our culture's image of a restaurant critic—like Kafka's Gregor Samsa in the body of a giant cockroach, only I was free to go outside. I now know that at any private dinner party at least one guest will ask if I'm planning to review our host's efforts. About 50 per cent of the time this person will also offer the first few lines of what he or she invariably calls the "write-up," usually beginning with the words: "My companion and I ...." Claim that you are just a guest, like all the others. Claim that you are not working. It doesn't help. If you're a restaurant critic, you've got a role and there isn't much to do but play it.

Here's a hint: it's comedy. To be a restaurant critic is to be, at heart, a buffoon. Nobody really takes restaurant critics seriously, not even themselves. Fran Lebowitz's suggested New Year's resolution for restaurant critics puts it succinctly enough: "Next year I'll get a real job." All entertainment writers field a certain amount of that kind of ribbing. "You mean they pay you to watch ballet?" comes the incredulous question. "You earn a living walking around art galleries?" This is nothing compared to the general amusement caused by the spectacle of a restaurant critic.

Restaurants are, of course, the places we go to perform the intimate animal act of eating in the presence of strangers. But it isn't this that makes people wink and nudge when they talk about restaurant reviewing. It's that there's something innately funny about earning a living by eating. The restaurant critic has pulled a fast one.

Hours may spin by as the critic crafts yet another review, carefully excising all the special, slimy non-words that come with the beat—delicious, tasty, appetizing or, most dog-eared cliché of all, "companion." But that's invisible toil. To outside eyes, all restaurant critics invert a natural law: people are supposed to exchange money for food. "Do you want me to pay you for breathing?" my mother used to enquire rhetorically when we discussed allowances and how much housework was required in exchange.

The truth is, yes, we would all like to be paid for breathing. But being paid for eating will do very nicely as second best. Except, of course, you don't get paid for eating. You get paid for writing about it.

I never got tired of eating in restaurants. I did get tired of writing reviews. Eventually I realized that restaurant reviewing was the laggardly part of my job. The free lunch had turned into a chore, one that I put off until the copy was due. So I stopped. For now.

EATING MY WORDS

Losing Ten Pounds

THE TWO-FACED DAY IS ALMOST HERE, THE MOMENT WHEN WE shut the door on the old year and stand peering into the new. Can we say goodbye to parts of the old self with the old year? Whispered voices say we can. Up comes the urge to recreate ourselves with the calendar, to seize the charged moment when the entire year lies ahead of us, still perfect and untouched. "Stop smoking," the voices say. "Don't be so messy." It is the hour of resolutions. Here is the message that takes first place: "Lose ten pounds."

I can't say how many New Year's Eves I made that resolution—twenty or perhaps twenty-five. I know it started before I was eighteen years old, because that year I had lost the ten pounds. I still didn't seem to be very thin, but the magic number showed up when I stepped on the scale. To mark this achievement, I resolved to give myself a break and lose just five pounds more.

Since I stopped dieting four years ago, I have puzzled over my longing to lose ten pounds. Like some past love affairs, it becomes more bizarre and improbable the longer you look at it. What was I doing? What made me decide that ten pounds separated me from the person I wanted to be? At the time, I thought I was demonstrating the power of my clear, intelligent will over my indolent body. Now I think of my desire to lose ten pounds as a revelation of my psychic life in symbolic language so clear it's embarrassing.

Visually, ten pounds is the amount of weight you appear to lose by standing up straight. It is also the amount of weight you appear to lose when your muscles are toned—130 flabby pounds look 10 pounds heavier than 130 fit pounds.

Medically, ten pounds doesn't exist. There is no condition that turns from health to pathology because you are ten pounds overweight. Ten pounds, in short, is nothing to fuss over. But fuss we do, because ten pounds is also everything.

When something is complete and all there, there are ten of them. We know this to be profoundly true because ten is the right number of fingers and toes to have. No other number will do; any more is excessive, any less is incomplete. There are ten commandments, and parables about ten talents, ten lamps, and ten virgins. Ten is the number of the cosmos, the paradigm of creation. J.C. Cooper writes in *An Illustrated Encyclopedia of Traditional Symbols* that ten "contains all numbers and therefore all possibilities."

Ten, in other words, is perfection. But a body can never be perfect. A body is a being, not a thing. It has its own consciousness, however little we may have access to it. It has a memory, and it has a genetic program. The idea of stepping back from the body, of trying to make it measure up to whatever ideal fashion might dictate, goes back in its modern form to 1918, when the first best-selling diet book, *Diet and Health with a Key to the Calories*, by Lulu Hunt Peters, appeared. The language of moral struggle is all there: we sin by eating and repent by dieting. Self-esteem depends on learning to control the appetite; weight loss is the proof of that control. "Every supposed pleasure in sin (eating) will furnish more than its equivalent of pain (dieting)," Peters wrote.

It won't do us any good to trace this odd relationship further into the Judeo-Christian past, nor to note how effectively advertisers have linked thin bodies with everything desirable. What we must understand is that the mind that resolves "this year I will lose ten pounds" has made a fundamental error. This is not apparent at first. The mind arbitrarily cuts down on the food supply. The body, surprised, continues to burn fuel at the same rate, and in a short time, ten pounds is gone. The mind is jubilant. It declares victory and goes out and buys a pair of jeans one size smaller. What it doesn't know is that the battle is already lost. For all but a tiny number of people, the weight will be back. Follow-up studies of dieters show a depressing truth: 95 per cent of people who lose weight gain it all back again within a year.

We are born with our metabolism already set. Active intervention from outside can speed it up, but not much. Similarly, our percentage of long-twitch and short-twitch muscles is 75 per cent determined at birth. The marathoner who tries to turn into a sprinter has embarked on an impossible task. Deciding to cut off food intake until the body measures up to a number on a scale is like playing an aggressive game of Monopoly with someone who already owns three-quarters of the board. You aren't going to win. Get a little more exercise, eat a little less fat, and you'll be at the thin end of your body's genetically determined range. Don't move around much, and eat fried food every day, and you'll be at the fat end.

The body that is starved becomes more economical with calories. Ten pounds gets harder to lose and easier to gain back. The more extreme and frequent the diets, the slower metabolism becomes. This is what gives the diet industry such brilliant growth opportunities: it creates its own customers. All but five per cent will gain the weight back and need even more help losing it the next time.

One of the most damning arguments against dieting I've seen comes from Neva Coyle, who wrote a book called *Overcoming the Dieting Dilemma*—it's worth a look if you have any lingering doubts about the futility of dieting. Coyle, once a devoted dieter— and founder of Overeaters Victorious, a support group for dieting Christians—so much wanted to be thin that she had intestinal bypass surgery. Six years of bad health followed; she was dying of malnutrition when her doctor ordered her to have the surgery reversed.

Losing weight has become what psychological researchers have called women's "normative obsession." Nine-year-old girls restrict their calorie intake. In *Fasting Girls: The Emergence of Anorexia Nervosa as a Modern Disease*, Joan Brumberg reports a *Glamour* magazine survey: "Of 33,000 women between the ages of 18 and 35, 75 per cent believed they were fat, although only 25 per cent were actually overweight. Of those judged underweight by standardized measures, 45 per cent still thought they were too fat."

The real meaning of our desire to lose ten pounds is this: it is the sign of a split self. If you want to lose ten pounds, then you are split between the imperfect body and the mind that seeks to perfect it. The mind, supposing itself to be either alone, or else just naturally in charge, sees the body, so close, so private, as the ideal arena for exerting control. First, it decides, we will lose ten pounds, and when that struggle is over, we will become perfect in other ways.

The body always wins. Hunger convinces us, and the more we struggle against it, the stronger it gets. Bulimic gorging is triggered, almost always, by dieting. The few who can hold out against their body's desire to eat are not winners. Despite the name of their disease—"anorexia" means loss of appetite—the little skeletons who walk among us are the hungriest of all.

I now weigh ten pounds more than I did when I first resolved to lose ten pounds. That puts me well within a normal range of weight for my height—although by my standards of twenty years ago, I'm elephantine. But I won't be resolving to lose ten pounds when the old year turns into the new. Perfection doesn't tempt me. I'm looking for balance.

Elixirs

THE FINAL MOMENTS ARE ALWAYS LIKE THIS: POPEYE IS pummelled, punched, twisted out of shape. Brutus, on his way to delivering the ultimate, killer blow, lumbers toward him. With his last drop of energy, Popeye squeezes a can of spinach until it pops open. He pours the primeval green ooze into his mouth. One chew, two chews, and down it goes. It takes a second to register on his gastric juices, then his body convulses with power. Turbines roar in his biceps. He's up like a tornado, inexhaustible, unbeatable, and strong to the "finich." Now that's an elixir. As far as I know, it's the only one that works, and it only works for Popeye.

Popeye's spinach is more famous by far than the little green plant of eternal life that the Sumerian hero Gilgamesh found at the bottom of the sea and lost to a water snake. That crimped can of spinach, its jagged lid forced open by the pressure of Popeye's fist, is better known than even the magic juice soma, the elixir of India and Iran, celebrated 3,500 years ago in Vedic hymns. Wine, mead, peyote, marijuana, gold dust: each one something we could swallow or smoke that would prolong life, grant vibrant health, give us the power of flight, lift us, in fact, out of the human plane and into the realm of the gods. As the world's most famous magic substance, Popeye's spinach is the perfect vehicle for exploring the landscape of elixirs.

Here are two things I can report after a tour through the territory: elixirs are essentially food in a hurry, and they don't work.

It's one of the strokes of genius in Popeye's creator, cartoonist Elzie Crisler Segar, that he chose spinach to explain the sailorman's phenomenal bursts of power. Spinach is a vegetable generally detested by children, especially when cooked, a vegetable that was the butt of popular joke when E.B. White wrote this caption for Carl Rose's *New Yorker* cartoon of a small boy at the dinner table: "It's broccoli, dear." "I say it's spinach, and I say the hell with it." But in the late 1920s, the fledgling science of nutrition had discovered vitamins and minerals. Spinach, because of its iron content, had gained a new status as a healthful food, the sort of food to put muscles on young arms.

Unlike Segar, the sages of fourth-century China didn't have the benefit of nutritional science. They were searching for what they thought of as an edible form of the Tao, or the life force. This was a very curious search, because we already have the life force in an edible form, and so did they. Except for table salt, thin sheets of gold on East Indian sweets and, for a small group of people in the southern U.S., clay, the only substances anybody eats are life forms.

While we're eating them, we call them food. Even vegetarian teeth rip through baby lettuce, bite carrots, and grind the living grain. It's all life eating life in a grand carnival—the Latin is *carne vale*, meaning, "flesh, goodbye." The worms get the dark moments at the bottom of the Ferris wheel, while up at the top, we picnic on any plant, animal, bird, fish, or fungus that catches our eye.

All of our food is life forms, all of it edible Tao. The truth of our relationship to food is easy to forget when you walk the aisles of packaged food in a supermarket, none of it either trapping soil in its roots or moving around on its own. In a garden, the life in food is simple, direct experience. In the thinnings from a row of radishes you can taste the small electric shock of something beyond flavour, still flowing.

Popeye's spinach, poured into Popeye's body, somehow ignites and runs through his veins like a great blast of life, like the distilled force of an entire field of radish thinnings. By comparison, food outside Popeye cartoons is disappointing in its immediate effects. We may well be what we eat, but you could hardly build a convincing case for that truism in a day, or even a week. Cheeseburgers, after all, turn into us—we don't turn into cheeseburgers.

People in general would prefer speedier and more dramatic effects from dinner, so they search for elixirs. But elixirs don't work. People have already spent centuries looking for elixirs. European alchemists borrowed the word from Arab alchemists, whose *al-iksir* was the name of the philosopher's stone, the magic substance that could transform base metals to gold and men to gods. In Greek, a related word, *xerion*, means a dry powder used for medicine and for alchemical transformations. Over the centuries, the word elixir has taken on the flavour of snake oil, the hint of nineteenth-century patent medicines like Dr. Walter's Digestive Elixir, brave warrior in the battle against dyspepsia. The one thing you're guaranteed at the bottom of every bottle is disappointment.

It's easy enough to smile at benighted children forcing themselves to eat green slime in the confident belief that canned spinach is the source of Popeye's power. Because they were unsophisticated enough to believe in spinach, they boosted consumption by 33 per cent in the first five years of Popeye's popularity, 1931 to 1936. And for what? Spinach alone will never make you strong enough to beat up your big brother. The soma drinkers who sang: "We have drunk the soma and become immortal," haven't survived to tell us exactly what soma might have been. (Scholars are not agreed on the merits of the thesis put forward by R. Gordon Wasson that soma was the juice of the *Amanita muscaria* mushroom. They do concur that at some point soma was replaced in ritual by less powerful substances, including rhubarb juice, which must have been every bit as disappointing as spinach.)

But it is the Chinese alchemists of the ninth century who may have gone most spectacularly off the track in searching for food that might feed us into godhood. One of the chief ingredients in their hundreds of elixirs was cinnabar, the blood-red ore of mercuric sulphide. The alchemists were convinced that a true elixir would be red, the colour of the final stage in the alchemical work. And cinnabar, when worked, yields mercury, the quicksilver element that anyone who ever got to play with the contents of a broken thermometer knows is the most "alive" of all the metals. Unfortunately, mercury is poisonous. Between 820 and 859, six emperors died from taking elixirs that promised eternal life, a toll that put a crimp in the Chinese alchemy trade from which it never recovered.

Death follows on the eating of mercury, and does so routinely enough to have given rise to this "Grahamism," (a term for grisly comic verse, of the sort found in Harry Graham's 1899 book *Ruthless Rhymes for Heartless Homes*):

Little Willie from the mirror,
Licked the mercury all off,
Thinking in his childish error,
It would cure the whooping cough.
At the funeral, his mother,
Weeping, said to Mrs. Brown,
Twas a chilly day for Willie,
When the mercury went down.

Knowing what I know, I would stick with spinach.

Breatharians: Eating Air

I HAVE BEEN KEEPING COMPANY WITH A TALL, THIN GENTLEMAN lately, name of Wiley Brooks. More precisely, I've been keeping company with the idea of Wiley Brooks, and with Wiley Brooks' one idea. For those who missed him the first time around, Brooks travelled the New Age lecture circuit in the early '80s, promoting the "breatharian" diet. Simplicity itself, the diet consisted of nothing to eat and nothing to drink, ever.

According to Brooks, breatharians feasted on oxygen and made all the liquids they needed inside their own bodies. Brooks claimed fourteen years of breatharian life, admitting to nothing more than a glass or two of mineral water with lemon juice in it whenever big-city pollution got the best of him. Drastic though it may have sounded, this diet left him, he claimed, "healthier, more energetic and happier than he ever dreamed possible." As a modest bonus for would-be breatharians attending lectures like the one in Vancouver's Robson Square media centre in October 1982, he also promised, in a poster for the event, to reveal "secrets of real happiness, joy, bliss, relationship, prosperity, consciousness and physical health."

Brooks was 47 when he spoke at Robson Square, black, six feet tall, 130 pounds. That's thin, but not nearly as thin as he would have been if it really had been fourteen years since he last ate.

Wiley Brooks made a living as a genuine, $100-a-ticket guru. He set up a Breatharian Institute in Larkspur, California, that attracted four hundred members. Okay, it was the '80s and nobody believed in limits. Besides, breatharianism fits easily into the well-accepted category of strange diets. It's the logical extension of all that advice on what foods to stop eating if you want to be thin. And surely if people can convince themselves to hand over their money and their fate to a guru called Wiley, it's just a small step to believing that he's learned how to live without food.

Once you've gotten over the initial disbelief, breatharianism offers practical advantages. Wave goodbye to Safeway. Spend the grocery money on clothes. No shopping, no loading the car, no unloading the car, no plastic grocery bags. Finally, enough space in the kitchen cupboards. No doing dishes ever again. Besides, breatharianism appeals to the rebellious streak in us all, the streak that goes right back to those old struggles with Mom on the other end of a spoon. Her message was: you've got to eat. She always won because ultimately she is absolutely right—at least until you turn into a breatharian and leave her high and dry.

But the people who came to the Breatharian Institute and followed its "transitional" diet of corn, fish, rice, chicken, and juice, were attracted by promptings older than these. Despite the distinctly modern trappings, Wiley Brooks was no new phenomenon. As Joan Jacobs Brumberg writes in *Fasting Girls: the Emergence of Anorexia Nervosa as a Modern Disease*, the credulous have always longed to believe in life without food. Brumberg's closest equivalent to Wiley Brooks is Anne Moore, "the Fasting Woman of Tutbury," who also fasted for a living. Moore, a domestic servant and the daughter of a labourer, stopped eating in 1808. In the first investigation of her claim, 117 people watched her day and night, and testified that she did not eat or drink. The resulting publicity brought visitors, who brought money: two hundred by one account, four hundred by another. Visitors gave her money because they thought she was holy. In fact, Moore fit right in with a tradition of fasting women that stretched back to the medieval saints.

She enjoyed five years of notoriety—which included having a wax likeness on display in a Boston museum—before a more carefully conducted watch disclosed the truth: her daughter Mary had been feeding her small bits of food hidden in handkerchiefs and in kisses.

Wiley Brooks' claim to living on air ended when he had a falling out with his girlfriend, Lavelle Lefler. Lefler revealed that the guru ate just like anyone else, only a little worse, since he had to get all his food on the sly from late-night groceries. His scam was considerably less sophisticated than Moore's; he seems to have put it together as he went along. Before 1980, when Brooks still lived in Venice, California, he claimed to live on a few light meals a week—to be a "social eater." As time went on, his claims got more outrageous. He maintained, for example, that food is a poison, and eating an addiction. (Inspiring, isn't it, how our lives can tell the truth even when our words don't? Who would deny that the sort of food Brooks ate is a poison of sorts, and that eating it leads to being addicted to high levels of sugar, salt, and fat?)

I think that Wiley Brooks flourished because of the deep-seated idea we have that there is something good about not eating. Poor, suffering humanity. One lot desperately scrabbling at the world to get enough to eat, the other trying to figure out if the calories from lunch really did get burned off in the aerobics class, and how much you can eat for dinner and still be "good."

Breatharians, dieters of all stripes, holy fasters: we are split in two by the age-old axe, cleaved into a body and a mind. As soon as we know about the split, we start the struggle, not for union, but for control. From our vantage point deep inside the mind, the struggle to control the body becomes the struggle of good over evil, of the spirit over the material world.

The war against the body is a long one, and it erupts in great excesses. For medieval ascetics, fasting was only one in an arsenal of "mortifications." Catherine of Siena also indulged in self-flagellation and scalding, and slept on a bed of thorns. To the split mind, physical suffering is the path to triumph, to the moment when we appear before the eternal judge, holding in our pure spirit a leash with a meek, emaciated body on the far end of it.

I like Wiley Brooks because in his bizarre claims he is a modern high-water mark in body hatred. This makes him a suitable guru for all who profit by our current separation from our bodies.

I'm waiting for the guru who comes singing wholeness—body and mind in harmony. Meanwhile, I plan to eat when I'm hungry.

Do Men Need Meat?

NO ONE WITH A LICK OF SENSE WOULD TRY TO CROSS AT THE intersection of food and gender without looking both ways first. So before we turn to our question—Do men need meat?—let us spend a moment with the knowledge that each man and each woman sees a different world. Even at times when it seems that only interplanetary travel holds an adequate explanation for the oddness of the opposite sex, we do well to remember that men are not right and women are not wrong, and vice versa.

So do men need meat? The short answer is no. Men don't need meat, women don't need meat, children don't need meat. If we are to take seriously the findings of diet researchers, meat in quantity is harmful. The net effect of a diet high in meat—and therefore in saturated fat—is higher rates of cancer and heart disease. In five years we may find ourselves asking: Should anyone be allowed to eat meat? Add a few more dietary studies to the accumulating pile and the U.S. Surgeon-General will eventually feel compelled to post warning notices in the meat display cases: "Eating meat is hazardous to your health. The danger increases with the quantity eaten."

Furthermore, it turns out that while red meat has high-quality protein that matches our own in its amino-acid structure, we don't need it. Nutritionists now believe that a good vegetarian diet poses no danger of protein deficiency.

But there is more to the picture of a man and a steak than just fat and protein. Let's put the man in a restaurant and give him a glass of red wine, and maybe a white shirt and a handsome tie. He looks far more virile than that other man, two tables over, eating a salad. He looks, in fact, like a man I often have dinner with.

In the backyard, the man and his steak are the hunter and his prey. Barbecuing is Dad's job, and he'll be cooking a steak. Meat is men's food because men have always hunted or tended the herd. Someone who eats meat spends his days running around with a spear and a bunch of other guys, hunting, or else he guards the flocks. Plant and fish foods are women's food. Women are people who spend their days rooting around in the ground. Women pick berries and dig for clams.

On average, hunting has more moments of high excitement than clamming. Wheat may nicely sustain the body until the next harvest, but compared to venison, bread is a dull meal indeed. Eat a deer and you eat the swiftness of the deer, the power coiled like springs in its legs. Men eat meat, so men are virile and powerful. Meat-eating separates the men from the women. She is cheese-cake; he is beefcake.

Like any cultural message that comes to us on a dinner plate, the relationship between men and meat has plenty of riders and exceptions. Lots of women eat meat, even if most of them aren't as memorable as Chicago bluesman James Cotton's girlfriend in "Hungry Country Girl," a carnivore with a hunger so vast that if she says she's hungry, it's a cow dead."

I'm told by a restaurateur who has been working the front of the house for thirty years that groups of women out for a dinner without the men will order rack of lamb, chateaubriand, red wine, and Drambuie. He bets with unsuspecting waiters on what food women without men will order, and wins. The firm conviction of Western culture is that eating meat is manly; meat belongs to men. By this scheme of reckoning, women, being more spiritual and finer creatures, should eat more feminine food. If we are to take George Eliot's word on it, Lord Byron once declared that the only foods delicate enough for a woman to eat in public were lobster salad and champagne.

Nowadays we see the fallacy of this reasoning, and none of us more keenly than the lobster. A death before dinner is a death before dinner, no matter how you slice it. But we continue in the pattern. In most cases, women who eat animal food at all eat chicken and fish; men eat meat. Without straining memory, I can think of five couples in which the woman is a vegetarian and the man is not. It is the standard pattern, and we would be surprised to see it reversed.

If men are hunks, then they are hunks of meat. The identity of men and meat is so central to us that along with meaning the substance of a matter, and the nutritive part of a nut as opposed to the shell, the word "meat" is a slang term for male genitals. It's a curious fact of the English language, by the way, that until the seventeenth century, "meat" applied to any food at all, animal flesh or not. "Butcher's meat" did not have the ring of redundancy that we hear in it, and a "meatless meal" was an oxymoron—if you were "meatless" you had no food at all.

Perhaps it's time to rework the meaning of meat again. For one thing, men's food is beginning to look like a bad evolutionary choice. Base your diet on meat and you may not be with us long. Base your diet on women's food—grains, fruits, and vegetables— and everyone from vegetarian evangelists to the local dietitian will tell you you're doing good things for your body. And in case you hadn't noticed, there's no such thing as men's food any more. By the reckoning of the old rules, all food is women's food, because all food is gathered. Men may have joined women as we fill our gathering bags at the neighbourhood market, but the activity is essentially the same. Expertise still resides in knowing where to find food rather than how to catch it, even if we now know where a good produce store is instead of knowing a good clam beach. And we still trade time for food, although we moderns first trade our time for money, then trade our money for food. Gathering remains sometimes pleasant, sometimes tedious, rarely riveting. Even in the meat department there are no electric moments of chase.

So why does that old thrill linger on in a New York steak, and roar as loudly as it ever did from raw beef? Eat a plate of carpaccio—raw tenderloin sliced transparently thin, capers, olive oil, black pepper and maybe a little mustard—and you'll get a jolt, a hit, a burst of energy that shouldn't be underestimated and can't be denied.

Do men need meat? The question, more clearly put, is this: Is the thrill of meat in some way particularly appropriate to men? Is there something important locked in red meat that men might forget if they don't keep eating it? Now that meat leads us back not to the hunt, but to the supermarket and the slaughterhouse, we might wonder if the long relationship between men and meat is now demeaning to men. Does a pork chop from a pig raised in a pig factory say anything about masculine power? Hasn't maleness always been more spacious than beef, more sublime than venison, wilder than wild boar?

We may find that in all these centuries we have fused two things—maleness and meat eating—that are only historically related. Think, if you like, of the early '60s, when men broke through the hair code and started growing out their crew cuts. Some adults—adult was almost a synonym at the time for people who had lost their grip on popular culture—used to complain that they couldn't tell the boys from the girls.

Turned out it wasn't so complicated after all.

Satiety

THE PLACE WHERE I LEARNED THAT BEING FULL IS NOT GOOD was in the basement cafeteria of the Hudson's Bay department store, some time in 1967. It was noon, and I was eating lunch with a fellow member of the store's teen fashion council. Early on Saturday mornings we met for lectures on foundation garments, wardrobe planning, and manicures. When the store opened, we sold clothes.

Under our identical mustard-coloured jackets and tartan beanies, we were not much alike. I'm from the east side. I was glad the uniform was compulsory. She would rather have worn her regular clothes. She was more fashionable, more slender, much more self-assured. She ate like a sparrow. I offered her some of my french fries and she declined. "I always like to leave the table feeling a little hungry," she said.

Nothing can put a crimp in your lunch like someone practising visible self-restraint. I had always assumed that the whole point of eating was to feel full. Now fullness had been revealed as coarse, plebeian, weak, and uncontrolled.

All that was nonsense, of course. There's nothing wrong with being full.

What we call fullness is no more than the digestive system telling the brain to stop eating. You feel full when liquefied food, flowing from the stomach through the pyloric sphincter and into the duodenum, triggers the release of certain hormones. The best known is cholecystokinin, usually called CCK; the list includes bombesin and somatostatin. Receptors in the brain note the presence of these hormones and turn off your appetite.

For such a neutral process, being full gets bad press. Slang cannot talk about being full without moans and mock cries of pain. We are stuffed to the gills, crammed, bloated, porked out. We couldn't eat another bite. When we are fed up, or when we have had a bellyful, we are not happy.

Even the staid pages of the *Oxford English Dictionary* disapprove of being full. "Satiety" comes from a Latin word meaning "enough." But the first meaning the *OED* lists for satiety is: "the state of being glutted or satiated with food; the feeling of disgust or surfeit caused by excess of food."

I think the reason we aren't comfortable with being full is that fullness is only a hair's breadth away from pain, nausea, self-disgust, and loathing. It isn't dislike of satiety we've got, but fear of nimiety. Nimiety is the state just beyond full, where pleasure turns into pain. We have all entered it at one time or another, and instantly wished we hadn't.

Paul Kulkosky, professor of psychology at the University of Southern Colorado, introduced the idea of nimiety at a New York Academy of Sciences-sponsored conference on food aversion in 1985. Kulkosky didn't make the word up; he just borrowed it. Nimiety, meaning excess and redundancy, is in the *OED*. It comes from the Late Latin *nimietas,* for "too much;" the first citation dates from 1564. It's unlikely that nimiety was ever a common word. By the nineteenth century it was already rare; certainly Coleridge thought he had to explain it when he used it. (The sentence, an ungenerous one, is: "There is a nimiety—a too-much-ness—in all Germans.") In the past, writers used nimiety to describe only the danger of sexual and spiritual gluts.

Kulkosky found an isolated use of the term while reading about thirst, and decided he had discovered a treasure. "The contribution I've made is this term nimiety," he says. "Some eating disorders can be described as failure to respond not just to satiety signals, but to nimiety signals."

We all eat to nimiety from time to time, and suffer for it. If we really over-indulge, we're likely to avoid the foods we stuffed with until the memory fades—a mechanism Kulkosky calls "the Thanksgiving effect." We have no examples of human beings eating until they explode. I suspect it's possible, all the same, if only because of Vincent Dethier's book *The Hungry Fly*, about his experiments with houseflies. If a certain nerve is cut, they will eat until they burst.

Why do we, with all our nerves intact, go blasting past satiety and into nimiety? Because it's easy. There is what Kulkosky calls "a grey zone" where pleasure ends and pain begins. This is partly because food doesn't reach the duodenum until about twenty minutes after you first start eating. Depending on how quickly you eat, the first of the satiety hormones may be released when you've already taken on more food than your body wants to digest.

Does that make my teen-fashion-council friend wise to keep hunger always with her?

Not really. Stephen Woods, professor of psychology and medicine at the University of Washington, says that a comfortable level of satiety is a learned response. "When we're eating something we've eaten in the past, we know when to stop," he says. "One reason children are so vulnerable to overeating is lack of experience." It is not distension of the stomach—which Woods suggests you visualize as a hot water bottle, collapsed when empty, tense and rounded when full—but the number of calories consumed, that brings us to satiety. Take, for ease of measurement, people fed on a liquid diet, like the ones sold in drugstores. At some level of fluid intake, they will report feeling full. If you tamper with the formula so that it delivers fewer calories, they will, for the first few days, continue to feel full with the old intake. Then their bodies adjust and they will drink, Woods says, "four or five times the amount" that had previously satisfied them, and report feeling no more full than before.

As a signal sent from the stomach to the brain, satiety is the opposite of hunger—a signal sent from the brain to the stomach. We don't have to listen, of course. And it may be that it's easier for the brain to get the stomach's attention than it is for the message of the stomach to filter into consciousness and lead us to put down the fork. If you are talking, if the food is unfamiliar, if it is a feast food that you are expected to eat in vast quantities, then nimiety awaits. But fullness isn't glut.

I suspect that we resist the message of satiety when we first hear it for other reasons. No matter how much we may fear hunger that won't go away, in our day-to-day experience, there isn't much that's better than the moment when we sit down to eat with our hunger sharp and the means to satisfy it at hand. The art of enjoying a meal is to stretch out the feeling of hunger as long as you can, to play with desire, massage it, coddle it, keep it alive by giving it variety. The danger is that while you're enjoying your hunger, you fail to hear satiety's voice.

Hunger, after all, is one of the ways we know we're alive. Even if the noble truths of the Buddha are looking nobler and more true to us by the minute—all life is suffering, all suffering arises from desire, the end of suffering is in the cessation of desire—we find desires excruciatingly hard to let go. Here is the disconcerting thing about being full. Suppose that every hunger we felt in life were simultaneously satisfied. Who would we find sitting in the vast stillness with nothing left to want?

Eating Contests

THE WINNER OF AN EATING CONTEST DEMONSTRATES POWER: A power of mind over body, of spirit over matter, of will over gag reflex. Nowhere has this been more clearly understood than among the Salish people of the B.C. and Washington coast, where they even have a word for it: *tsatlad*, or *tsatlsqulalitut*—eating power.

Powers played an important role in Coast Salish culture. There were many kinds, including, but not limited to, the powers of a shaman, and any adult ought to have one or more. A person with eating power ate normally most of the time. But when challenged or challenging, the same person would eat vast quantities of food without showing the slightest sign of discomfort.

Mainstream Western culture knows two kinds of eating contest: formal and informal. Formal contests divide again into two: the folk events, like the Silver Crik Festival Banana Split Eating contest in Garrettsville, Ohio, and the professional leagues, best exemplified by the people who show up in the *Guinness Book of World Records*.

Until 1990, when Guinness dropped its gluttony category, this was the place to look for the feats of professional eaters. The most accomplished record setter was Englishman Peter Dowdeswell who, as of 1986, held 279 world eating records, including: a pound of cheddar cheese in 1 minute, 13 seconds; 13 raw eggs in 1 second;

38 soft-boiled eggs in 75 seconds; 3 pounds of shrimp in 3 minutes, 10 seconds; 2 pounds of strawberries in 12.95 seconds; 3 pounds of potatoes in 1 minute, 22 seconds; 5 pounds, 12 3/4 ounces of sausage meat in 4 minutes, 29 seconds. Dowdeswell's wife held the women's ale-drinking record. His son Tony was world cockle-eating champion and world ice-cream eating champion, and a son-in-law had scarfed down 3 pounds, 12 ounces of chicken in 12 minutes, 37 seconds, to become world king of chicken-eating. The biggest puzzle for me is why Guinness would group these feats under the heading "gluttony." I thought gluttons were supposed to enjoy themselves. In fact, I thought the whole point of gluttony, the reason it's one of the seven deadly sins and not just something you can take or leave, is that it's enjoyable. Where is the pleasure in downing 13 slimy raw eggs in one gulp?

Very few of us are inclined, like Donna Maiello, to eat 100 yards of spaghetti in 27.75 seconds, and even fewer make sure that there's someone standing by with a stopwatch. But we are all familiar with informal eating contests, and even more familiar with times when people who eat normally most of the year stuff themselves at enormous ritual dinners.

The human stomach can expand. It has folds in it that flatten out as the food inside presses against the stomach walls. This is a lucky thing, too, because for thousands of years, our bodies were the only food-storage containers we had. Even after we took up agriculture, and built storehouses for grain, there were fat and lean times of the year. Some German country inns still put on a slaughter festival menu in the fall—a remnant of the days when animals that could not be fed over the winter were slaughtered when the weather turned cold. In Christian Europe, the slaughter was the beginning of the feasting season, which lasted until Lent—the fasting season—which ended with spring chicken and lamb and the first edible greens.

The ability to go beyond the normal limits of the stomach rouses the temptation to see just how far beyond we can go. So small boys try to break their own pancake-eating records, egged on by this logic: the more you can eat, the bigger you are. Add an opponent to the breakfast table, and you've found a way to discover which boy is the bigger boy. Jay Jacobs, a former New York restaurant critic for *Gourmet* magazine, tells the story of two such eating contests in his book, *A Glutton for Punishment: Confessions of a Mercenary Eater*. In the first, Jacobs and a M. du Bellon, his neighbour in the small Provençal town where Jacobs and his wife lived, engage in combat over who can eat the most snails. Jacobs reels away in defeat after they've each eaten 11 dozen. Then another neighbour, a M. Orgeas, throws down a more subtle gauntlet, a dinner invitation. "Even before the first course was served, it was obvious that M. Orgeas had every intention of taking my measure," Jacobs writes. "I knew I was engaged in another *mano a mano*, like it or not, and scrupulously kept pace with him." The meal Jacobs consumes is: a huge appetizer course of cold meat, a whole chicken apiece, roast beef, a ragout of meatballs, vegetables, salad, floating islands, and cheese—and bread and wine with all of the above, of course. Driven to hallucinations by this excess, Jacobs goes home to sleep it off, and then hides out for a few days "mortified by my gastronomic trouncing chez Orgeas."

Coast Salish eating contests were as personal as the ones Jacobs entered. The difference is that only one person or one team ate, and it was always the guests. The object was, literally, to eat the host out of house and home. Drop by my house at the right time, and this could take less than 15 minutes - which was of course, the point. The eater's boast: "My power can consume everything you own." The host's implicit reply: "I am so rich, I have so much food, that I can feed your eating power until it can't eat any more"— which is a serious malfunction in an eating power.

"All of a man's property and his wives and children might be forfeit if he lost in such a situation," writes Marian Wesley Smith, in her 1940 ethnographic study *The Puyallup-Nisqually*. Smith notes that it was not just the amount of food eaten that was extraordinary, but the style with which it was eaten: "After consuming the food and while eating, the person showed no extra puffiness nor bunches on his body or under his clothes." So when three old men came to challenge one of Smith's informants at a feast, they talked and joked among themselves as they ate four entire meals apiece. They stopped short when he still had a half a side of beef left, and blamed their defeat on the watermelon he'd served for dessert. Too much water. Three years later, they came back for a return match. After an entire yearling steer, potatoes, rice, beans, bread, and fruit, they conceded defeat. There is no record of what, if anything, they lost.

Then there's the story of the old man who, in his youth, had boasted of his eating power around some white settlers. When challenged, he sat down and ate two sides of beef—a cow, in other words—and washed it down with a barrel of water. "They were satisfied," Smith's informant says.

I would have been more nervous than satisfied watching a man of normal size eat a cow—calmly, chewing well as he went, possibly making jokes and taking side bets, showing no signs of discomfort. The barrel of water I can accept, somehow. But where did the cow go? The Puyallup-Nisqually people who talked to Smith in the 1930s would have said that the man's power ate the cow. That's at least as reasonable as the idea that it all fit in his stomach. Of course, physics tells us that the cow and the man are both just collections of atoms, which is to say tiny bits of matter and a whole lot of empty space.

Maybe Coast Salish power eaters knew some way to restructure the food so it became immensely compact. Maybe not. But if a cow disappears into a man, and the man does not blow up, like Mr. Creosote in Monty Python's *The Meaning of Life,* then I, for one, would like an explanation. If it isn't the stomach, what gives?

Why Backwash Is Dirty

MAINSTREAM NORTH AMERICAN CULTURE DOES NOT SIT UP nights worrying about the spiritual purity of its food. If it's free of harmful bacteria, if there are no visible bugs, mouse droppings, or stray hairs, then you can eat it. Some foods are not widely popular, but nothing is forbidden.

Two great pillars of thought support this attitude. The first, with us now for almost two thousand years, comes from the New Testament, Book of Mark, chapter seven: "Whatever goes into a man from outside cannot defile him, since it enters, not his heart but his stomach, and so passes on. What comes out of a man is what defiles a man." The second, a mere century old, is knowledge of bacteria. We may not be able to prevent the majority of our broiler chickens from going to market contaminated by either salmonella or campylobacter—both of them capable of causing nasty illness. But we know what these bacteria are and how to kill them in the course of cooking the chicken. We know enough to believe that we understand what makes food dirty.

Here is the big exception. Any child over the age of six knows that all you have to do to protect your pop from a predatory older sibling is spit in it. Or, more elegantly, you can take a large mouthful, swill it back into the glass, and say "backwash." No matter how appealing your soft drink may have been seconds earlier, no one but you will touch it now.

The polluting power of backwash does not run afoul of the New Testament code. Nor is it a question of bacterial contamination. A healthy person's saliva won't make you sick. You are far more at risk from a medium-rare hamburger—which may be contaminated by E. coli—and millions of those are eaten every day. Nonetheless, the presence of someone else's saliva is enough to make food dirty. There is, by the way, a definitive test for dirty food. As soon as you register the source of pollution, invisible hands reach for the valve that controls your hunger and shut it off. Backwash passes the test. So what makes backwash dirty?

The most convincing answer so far was supplied by British anthropologist Mary Douglas in her book *Purity and Danger: An Analysis of the Concepts of Pollution and Taboo*. Douglas points out that human beings make their way through the world by filtering only a few sense impressions from the thousands that are available to us in each second of our lives. We don't just see our reality, we select it. By ordering our experience, we make the parts that don't conform to our order dirty. So, Douglas writes, "Shoes are not dirty in themselves, but it is dirty to place them on the dining-table; food is not dirty in itself, but it is dirty to leave cooking utensils in the bedroom, or food bespattered on clothing; similarly, bathroom equipment in the drawing room; clothing lying on chairs; outdoor things indoors; upstairs things downstairs; under-clothing appearing where over-clothing should be, and so on."

Dirt, to use an old definition, is matter in the wrong place. "Dirt is never a unique, isolated event," Douglas writes. "Where there is dirt, there is system." From this foundation, she goes on to analyze the Jewish dietary laws, known as the laws of *kasruth*, which determine which food is kosher, or fit to eat. Her analysis is too long and too subtle to reproduce here. But the bones of her argument may be rendered this way: the Jewish world is founded on a three-part division into water, land, and air. Clean animals are the animals that act most appropriately in each element. Things that move in the air should have two legs and fly with wings. Things that swim in water should have fins and scales. The proper land animals for a herding people to eat are those that most closely resemble sheep and cattle. In other words, they should have a cloven hoof and chew the cud. Pigs, to take the best-known example of an unclean animal, have a cloven hoof but don't chew the cud. And it is this fact that renders the pig unfit to eat, not its diet or its personal habits, nor any early intimations of the dangers of trichinosis. "The sole reason for its being unclean," Douglas writes, "is its failure as a wild boar to get into the antelope class." Douglas observes that pollution concerns are strongest in societies that feel threatened. A classic working of this rule occurred when the Romans exiled the Jews from Palestine in the first century CE. In response, rabbinical interpretation of dietary law became much more strict.

So how do these ideas apply to backwash?

In the first place, saliva is always a problem when the question of purity arises, because it falls within the class of bodily secretions, along with blood, sperm, tears, and feces, all of them hedged about with power and terror.

You have only to think of a child sucking on a jawbreaker, taking it out to see how the colour changes, and popping it back in, to know that our worries about saliva are relatively mild. By contrast, the Coorgs, a small Hindu caste with a strong set of food purity rules, would find the same child and jawbreaker—the child, in effect, eating its own saliva—disgusting.

One Coorg myth tells how a goddess came to be in a subordinate position to her two brothers. After she had beaten them in several contests of strength and intelligence, they tricked her into removing a betel nut from her mouth and popping it back in again. "Once she realized she had eaten something which had once been in her own mouth and was therefore defiled by saliva...she accepted the full justice of her downfall," Douglas writes.

For most North Americans it isn't our own saliva, or even saliva in general that bothers us. It's other people's saliva. And we aren't even consistent in that. Under limited circumstances we will kiss other people and willingly mix our saliva with theirs. But food we have marked as ours is, by extension, already part of our body. And our way of seeing ourselves is as closed systems. We are ruggedly individual, alone, complete in ourselves. We have borders, boundaries. When pollution comes to our food, it comes from other people; what is ours, is clean. We understand completely what New Zealand short story writer Katherine Mansfield meant when she wrote in her journal under the heading Living Alone, "Even if I should, by some awful chance, find a hair upon my bread and honey—at any rate it is my own hair."

We are the people of the single-portion pack and the individually wrapped cheese slice. We are the society that elevated the phrase "untouched by human hand" into a byword for purity. The threat to our system that gives backwash its power is this: the mouth is the gateway to the body, but the gate can't be kept shut. We have no choice but to eat. Three times a day we reiterate the fact that our life depends on other lives. We breathe in and out, eat and excrete, continually taking the world in, transforming it, and sending it out again. All around us, our families and friends permeate our lives. We grieve at their sorrows, pop up in their dreams, wander with them through common unconscious terrain. We are always much closer to one another than the fiction of the rugged individual would have it. No wonder the guard at the gate is nervous. No backwash, please.

Forbidden Fruit

OUR STORY OF THE FALL SAYS THAT A WOMAN ATE FORBIDDEN fruit and that's why we're in the mess we're in. Your kid needs braces? Your cat's at the vet again? You look around and see mindless violence, random suffering? You've noticed the bruise in the apple? The phenomenon of decay? The book of Genesis says you may blame Eve. She ate forbidden fruit and brought suffering into the world. Adam ate too, of course, but she ate first and gave it to him.

It's all very well to argue that religious stories no longer count in our scientific world. Eve is still much in our minds. Everyone knows that Eve's fruit is the apple; every wit I meet wants to know if my husband's name is Adam. Anyone who reads women's magazines sees her shadow. Women are the guilty sex, carriers of an exquisite guilt that stretches back to the most momentous snack in the history of Western civilization.

We can never assign a name to Eve's fruit. The story of The Fall tells us only that it came from the tree of the knowledge of good and evil. Logic tells us that it was more likely a fig than an apple, but the first rule of stories is that you can't trust logic to fill in the details. Terence McKenna, in a book called *Food of the Gods: The Search for the Original Tree of Knowledge*, argues that a forbidden fruit not only existed in the real world, but was psycho-active. His candidate is *Psilocybe cubensis*, the magic mushroom that grows in cattle dung.

"Psilocybin's main synergistic effect seems ultimately to be in the domain of language," he writes. "It excites vocalization; it empowers articulation; it translates language into something that is visibly beheld. We literally may have eaten our way to higher consciousness."

I have a special interest in the story of forbidden fruit because I share a name with Eve. I was twenty-one when an English boyfriend, who pronounced my given name, Evelyn, as Eve-lyn, dropped the -lyn. I lost the boyfriend, kept the name. At the time I didn't think much about the connection with the biblical Eve. Lately I've come to think of her as a role model. After all, who better exemplifies changed consciousness through food?

That's not to say I like the story as it's most often told. What an odd place this paradise is, with talking snakes and a keeper who is given to prohibitions and fits of temper. The hardest question of all is what we should think of this omnipotent, omniscient Creator who first points out the tree and then forbids it. He seems to be a Creator afraid of His own creatures. "Behold, the man has become like one of us, knowing good and evil," He tells the assembled angels. To forestall the next possibility, that Adam would "put forth his hand and take also of the tree of life, and eat, and live for ever," He kicks the miscreants out of paradise.

In *Answer to Job*, Carl Jung argues that we might consider Jehovah as unconscious and His rages and acts of vengeance as the behaviour of Someone with limited self-knowledge. "It is as if someone started a bacterial culture which turned out to be a failure," Jung writes. "He might curse his luck, but he would never seek the reason for the failure in the bacilli and want to punish them morally for it. Rather, he would select a more suitable culture medium."

Adam and Eve in the garden is one of humanity's basic story patterns, woven all over the world in a hundred variations. Mircea Eliade's *Encyclopedia of Religion* will tell you that none of the gods in the world's stock of Fall stories are much better behaved. Eliade's article on The Fall also makes it clear that the human transgressions involved are wonderfully arbitrary. The essentials are: a golden age in the past, an ancestor who makes a mistake, and a much-diminished present reality.

In Burkina Faso, Eliade writes, "the vault of heaven was origi nally within man's reach, but when a woman who touched the vault with a load of wood she was carrying on her head asked God to move it out of her way, he moved it so far that he abandoned mankind to death." The Dogon of Mali believe that God separated heaven from earth and made men mortal because he was irritated by the noise of women crushing millet. A Southeast Asian myth tells us that the first man was equipped in paradise with shovels that turned the earth over by themselves. He got drunk and neg- lected to feed his tools, which revolted, and by all appearances work against us still. Another Southeast Asian story points to the primordial couple's refusal to dive head first into a well when commanded to do so by the god Ong Ndu as the reason we expe- rience suffering, old age, and death.

Forbidden fruit, it turns out, is just like so much trim on a house. You can take it off and replace it with any other example of human disobedience, disrespect, or stupidity and the structure of the story changes not at all. Still, it's our trim. And rolling down through centuries of Judaism, Christianity, and Islam it has fed a tendency to group women, fruit, and sex together and find them dangerous, frightening, bad, and furthermore, to blame. From inside the culture with the apple we can only wonder what it would be like to live in a society that lost paradise because a man got drunk.

Suppose Jehovah had commanded Adam and Eve to jump head first into a well and they had disobeyed, causing us to get head colds and runs in our stockings. Now there is a Fall we could live with. Other than act properly should the occasion ever arise again, what could you possibly be expected to do about it? Instead we are hedged about by forbidden fruit. We have countless opportunities to sin, depending on what it is our background tells us is forbidden: pleasure in sex, pleasure in food, or pleasure in both.

Meanwhile, the story has become hopelessly muddled. As children we learn about a talking snake and an apple. As we lose our own innocence we learn that what happened in the garden is the original smutty joke. The first sin was the decision to disobey and its first expression was eating, but, for us, original sin has become a code word for sex, and therefore reliably funny.

We may in time learn to tell the story a different way. In *Adam, Eve, and the Serpent*, Elaine Pagels writes of early gnostic Christians who saw the snake as a hero and Jehovah as a tyrannical demigod trying in jealousy to keep man away from knowledge of his true self.

No matter how much we might eventually change the interpretation, I hope we keep the detail about the fruit. Eating is a bold metaphor for learning: we take in food, react with it chemically, and change. Our understanding of the world is not the same after the first taste of zabaglione, or for that matter, burned porridge.

If the apple must go—too freighted with Eve's guilt and God's anger—perhaps we might consider blood oranges as a replacement. The first one I ever ate, small and unpromising from the outside, fell back from the knife blade to reveal two ruby circles ringed in white and orange, bleeding a red juice.

Any fruit worth prohibiting should contain an element of surprise. We bite into it, eyes closed, taste, chew, swallow, and open our eyes on a new world.

Eating to Live
or Living to Eat?

I AM FED UP WITH THE PHRASE "I DON'T LIVE TO EAT, I EAT TO live." If you say it around me, duck. I can no longer be responsible for my actions.

What commonplace of the English language is more repugnant? What statement of wrong-headedness is at the same time so smug and so much applauded?

Saints and mystics eat to live, or so we imagine, since no one who lived to inhale oysters and caviar has been canonized by any church outside the gastronomic faith. Cowboys from Roy Rogers to Clint Eastwood poke cows, eat beans, and don't waste time thinking about eating. Ambitious, driven, type-A personalities fuel up on food. Calories in, calories out, then on to more important things. You might as well be putting gas in a car.

By contrast, few people are willing to declare that they live to eat. American food writer James Beard, who died in 1985 after releasing American cooks from the greasy arms of Miracle Whip and Velveeta, lived to eat. He had gargantuan appetites and a gargantuan physique.

I would submit that Beard and Clint Eastwood fall equally far from the mark. Both sides of the "eat to live/live to eat" coin are spurious, and those who hoard it in their mental savings are poorer than they know.

Here's a short history of this obnoxious phrase:

"I eat to live" is supposed to have entered the collective Western mind through Socrates. I hope that isn't true, because I hold a high, if rather hazy, regard for him and don't want to have to revise my opinion. Mind you, like everything Socrates is supposed to have said, this is reportage, hearsay. Diogenes Laertius, who wrote his *Lives and Opinions of Famous Philosophers* two hundred years after Socrates died, has it simply as: "He used to say that other men lived to eat, but that he ate to live." Plutarch, filing his copy 250 years later still, wrote that Socrates said: "Bad men live that they may eat and drink, whereas good men eat and drink that they may live."

We can only suspend judgment on the first count. But we can let the old philosopher off on the second. Socrates was too smart to have said that.

In ancient Greece, just like here and now, evil people live to gain power over others and hurt them, not to eat and drink. What a heaven this world would be if dictators, mass murderers, and petty tyrants could be bought off with truffles and champagne.

Molière wrote the phrase into *The Miser (L'Avare)* in 1668. Henry Fielding translated the play and the phrase into English sometime between 1729 and 1737. In Act III, Harpagon, the miser, seizes on "We must eat to live and not live to eat" with delight, proposing to have the words engraved over his hall chimney. The sentiment does, after all, lend credence to his theory that when ten guests are invited there need only be food for eight, since too much is always provided. And what a meal: "Such things as people can't eat much of, and that cloy them immediately; some good pease-porridge, pretty fat, with a pie in a pot, well garnished with chestnuts...."

By 1733, when it pops up in Benjamin Franklin's *Poor Richard's Almanac,* "I eat to live" had taken on the smug moral superiority it has today. In *Bartlett's Familiar Quotations* it appears as "Eat to live and not live to eat," happily ensconced among Franklin's other mental gemstones of similar lustre. There's 1738's: "If you would not be forgotten, as soon as you are dead and rotten, either write things worth reading, or do things worth the writing." And who could resist the pithier and poetically more resolved, "Little strokes fell great oaks" of 1750? The temptation is to quote and quote, but it's time to move on.

The rotten smell at the core of "I don't live to eat, I eat to live" is this: Living to eat is not the opposite of eating to live, no more than denial of pleasure from food is the opposite of gluttony. Both are defective attitudes, alike in their deficiency. The true opposite of both of them is eating well.

"I eat to live," insists that we compare eating, which is part of living, to all of life, and find on comparison that eating is the lesser of the two. Right: the whole is greater than its parts. But we don't spend our time grandly "living" so much as we spend it engaged in specific activities. Break living down into its components and you get rather less elevated statements—"I eat to drive to work," "I eat to sleep," "I eat to watch television," "I eat to brush my teeth," "I eat to read," "I eat to shop," and even: "I eat to eat."

Our best examples of being human and alive tell us that the present moment, however we may use it, is the only moment we can live in. Sometimes, in the present moment, we eat. To live at the table requires the senses. To marshal, educate, and heed the senses requires concentration.

Let us turn now to a story from the life of St. Theresa of Avila, founder of the Carmelite order of nuns, who rose to sainthood in sixteenth century Spain. Late in her career she visited a monastery, and ate dinner there with the abbot. He had put aside the usual simple dietary habits of the order, and in honour of his guest, served roast partridge. The saint dived in up to her elbows. The abbot, taken aback, chided her for her obvious enjoyment, saying that it was unseemly for a woman of prayer to show such gusto at the table. St. Theresa replied: "When it's prayer time, pray. When it's partridge time, partridge."

Paying attention to food is harder now than it was when Theresa ate her partridges. Not only are our minds fragmented by the pushes and pulls of daily life, but if we pay attention to food, we run headlong into hard issues. Who wants their reverie over fried eggs to be interrupted by visions of caged hens? Who wants to eat a California tomato knowing that it's an industrial vegetable, genetically tailored for transport, chemically grown, and raised solely for profit by large farm corporations?

One way out of this is to close your eyes and repeat "I eat to live," like a mantra. Enough already with the damned chickens. We're all suffering one way or another. The problem with this strategy is that, as far as we know, consciousness is not on a dimmer switch to be turned up and down at will. You can't decide to close your mind to one part of the web of food and then expect your senses to embrace the rest.

Some people have good reason to eat without pleasure and with minimal thought. Illness and age can steal our taste buds. Sensory endowments differ; some of us are born with less than the normal ability to taste food. It is a genuine handicap. As Jean-Anthelme Brillat-Savarin, nineteenth-century French lawyer and the father of gastronomy, writes: "The empire of taste may also have its blind and its deaf subjects." The rest of us eat and live, both. To say "I eat to live" or "I live to eat" is to refuse the whole and live only in one of its parts. If people must do this, then they must. I see no reason to be proud of it.

Acknowledgements

Thanks go, first of all, to all those who generously shared their food knowledge with me, either in conversation or in their books. And particular thanks to the librarians at the Vancouver Public Library for helping me navigate the vast world of food.

Daphne Gray-Grant was features editor at *The Vancouver Sun* when I began writing these essays and her clarity, encouragement and sage writing advice made them far better than they would otherwise be. Michael Scott, Peter Wilson, and Max Wyman, who succeeded Daphne as Saturday Review editors, laughed at my jokes and put up with my tardiness and histrionics.

Thanks to Arthur Black for being the greatest of fun to work with, and for writing the charming foreword, and to *Basic Black's* producer, Chris Straw, quite possibly the nicest person ever to work in radio.

Jaimie Hubbard, Life editor Dianne deFenoyl and Saturday Post Food editor Sheilagh McEvenue helped sharpen the stories that ran in *The National Post*. Jim Sutherland and Nick Rebalski did the same for the stories that ran in *The Mix*.

At Whitecap, Robert McCullough gave the book his support and Robin Rivers kept it on track without actually nagging. Kathy Evans edited the manuscript with precision and care, saved me from several errors, and made useful suggestions. Lee Anne Smith prepared the index, with assistance from Kim Feltham.

Beth McTavish read the manuscript and made astute and kind suggestions. Gayle Chronister, dear friend and commiserator, gave invaluable moral support. Carol Volkart, Marla Britton and Louie Ettling all read stories and told me what they thought of them. Mary Balomenos, my partner in Yoga on 7th, took on more than her share of teaching duties to give me time to work. Thanks to all of you.

As ever, thanks to Alan for his steady love.

Index

RECIPE INDEX

BREAD

Fearless Pizza Dough, 7

CONDIMENTS

Faster Than Going to the Store Ketchup, 139

Fig Preserves with Lime and Mint, 78

DESSERTS

Chocolate Cake, Aunt Esther's, 93

Chocolate Fudge, 46

Favourite Christmas Pudding, 52-53

Lemon Ice–Cream Bars Dipped in Dark Chocolate, 25

Mangoes and Sticky Rice, 73–74

Maple Syrup Chocolate Chip Cookies, 58

Rum Sauce, 53

MAIN DISHES

Chicken with Forty Cloves of Garlic, 12

Coconut Milk Mussels as Hot as You Want Them, 87

Curried Lentils and Sweet Potatoes, 128

Gingered Fish Tacos with Guacamole, 98

VEGETABLES

Grilled Artichokes, 69

GENERAL INDEX

Adams, Edith, 13–16

Alford, Jeffery, 72

Andrews, Jean, 84

Appert, Nicholas, 18

Artichokes, 65–68

Backwash
  food purity and, 213–16

Baker, Norma Jean. *See* Monroe, Marilyn

Barry, Dave, 123

Batterberry, Michael and Ariane, 113

Beard, James, 9, 221

Beard, Harry, 31

Bertolli, Paul, 37

Breatharians, 197, 199

Brillat–Savarin, Jean–Anthelme, 224

Brooks, Wiley, 197–200

Burros, Marian, 157

Butterfat
  milk production and, 170–73

Canning
  history of , 18–19

Capsaicin, 83

Castelli, Angelo–Charles and Catherine A., 65

Celery
  history of, 34–37

Cheezies
  history of, 140–42

Chickens
  egg production and, 163–64
  production of, 158
  symbols of, 162

Chicken rings, 166, 168–69

Chicken with forty cloves of garlic
  origin of, 9

Chilies
    measuring heat of, 83–84
    masochism and, 84–85
Chocolate
    chemical composition of, 90–91
    history of, 89–90
Christmas pudding. *See* Plum pudding
Coffee, cat–poop. *See* Luwak coffee
Cookery, 8
Cost, Bruce, 97
Cotton candy
    history of, 132–33
    making, 131
    names for, 131

David, Elizabeth, 75, 81
Davidson, Alan, 49
Duguid, Naomi, 72

Eating contests
    Coast Salish culture and, 209, 211–12
    records in, 209–210, 211
Eggs
    production of, 161–62, 163–64
Elixirs
    search for, 193–96

Famine
    children and, 178–79
    world economy and, 179–80
Fennel, 35, 37
Figs, 75–77
Food groups
    categories in, 31–32
    prototypes of, 30–31, 32–33
Food preservation. *See* Canning
Food production, 157–60, 175–77
Forty
    significance of, 9–10
Four
    significance of, 31
Fudge
    history of, 43
    making, 43–45
Fungi. *See* Mushrooms

Garabaghi, Vilma Pesciallo, 174
Garlic, 8, 10–11

Gin
    history of, 115–19
Ginger
    chemical composition of, 95
    history of, 96–97
Grigson, Jane, 67

Hess, John and Karen, 176
Hesser, Amanda, 66
Hyam, Nathan, 73

"I live to eat"
    history of, 222–23

Junk food
    effects of, 147–48

Kadans, Joseph, 97
Ketchup
    history of, 137–39
Kitchen rage, 26, 28–29

Lemon meringue pie
    about, 21–22
    history of, 23–24
Lentils
    kinds of, 126
    origin of, 125
Lindsay, Anne, 136, 139
Luwak coffee, 120–21
Luwaks, 122

Mangoes
    Indian culture and, 99, 100, 101
    types of, 99
Marianai, John, 43, 91
Marshmallows
    history of, 150–52
McKenna, Terence, 217
McKie, Roy, 31
Meat eating
    gender and, 202–204
Medlars
    appearance of, 109
    bletting and, 109–10
    how to eat, 111
Monroe, Marilyn, 65, 67
Mouth surfing, 84–85

Mushrooms
  commercial production of, 106
  growth habit of, 103, 105, 106
  types of, 104

Nimiety, 206–207

Ott, Jonathan, 90

Pederson, Pat, 16
Peppers, Hot. *See* Chilies
Pheasants
  historical references to, 114
Pheasant under glass
  origin of, 113–14
  symbolism of, 112
Pigs
  gluttony and, 40–41
  popular culture and, 39
Plum pudding, 48–51
Priestley, Joseph, 154
Puckett, Susan, 17

Rannie, William, 61
Restaurant critics
  life as, 185–88
Root, Waverly, 108, 109, 114
Round food, 167
Rye whisky
  history of, 60–62

Satiety
  learned response and, 207
  physiology of, 205–206
Soda water
  history of, 154–55
Speigel, Robert, 85
Spit. *See* Backwash
Sticky rice
  cooking, 72–73
Stewart, Martha, 13, 14–15, 16

Ten
  significance of, 190
Thompson, Brenda, 14
Thorne John, 9
Toaster
  history of, 81–82
Twinkies
  history of, 145–146

Utah 52–70. *See* Celery

Visser, Margaret, 172

Waters, Alice, 37
Weaver, William Woys, 24, 51
Woodstove cooking, 57